Urban regeneration through partnership

A study in nine urban regions in England, Wales and Scotland

Michael Carley, Mike Chapman, Annette Hastings, Karryn Kirk and Raymond Young

The POLICY PRESS

Regeneration Box

First published in Great Britain in May 2000 by

The Policy Press
34 Tyndall's Park Road
Bristol BS8 1PY
UK

Tel no   +44 (0)117 954 6800
Fax no +44 (0)117 973 7308
E-mail tpp@bristol.ac.uk
http://www.policypress.org.uk

© The Policy Press and the Joseph Rowntree Foundation 2000

Published for the Joseph Rowntree Foundation by The Policy Press

ISBN 1 86134 250 0

Michael Carley is a Professor, **Mike Chapman** is a Lecturer and **Karryn Kirk** is a Research Associate, all at the School for Planning and Housing, Heriot-Watt University, Edinburgh. **Annette Hastings** is Lecturer in Urban Regeneration and **Raymond Young** is Honorary Senior Research Fellow, both at the Department of Urban Studies, University of Glasgow.

The **Joseph Rowntree Foundation** has supported this project as part of its programme of research and innovative development projects, which it hopes will be of value to policy makers, practitioners and service users. The facts presented and views expressed in this report are, however, those of the authors and not necessarily those of the Foundation.

The statements and opinions contained within this publication are solely those of the authors and contributors and not of The University of Bristol or The Policy Press. The University of Bristol and The Policy Press disclaim responsibility for any injury to persons or property resulting from any material published in this publication.

The Policy Press works to counter discrimination on grounds of gender, race, disability, age and sexuality.

Cover design by Qube Design Associates, Bristol
Front cover: top left photograph kindly supplied by www.johnbirdsall.co.uk; top right photograph of Perthcelyn Estate, Wales, kindly supplied by Katy Bennett, Department of Geography, University of Durham
Printed in Great Britain by Hobbs the Printers Ltd, Southampton

Contents

Acknowledgements

The research team is particularly grateful to the hundreds of urban regeneration practitioners, community representatives, policy advisers and politicians in England, Wales and Scotland who gave generously of their time to assist this research. Unfortunately, they are too numerous to name.

We are also grateful to the Joseph Rowntree Foundation for supporting this research intellectually and financially, and particularly to John Low for his advice and support. John chaired the Project Advisory Group whose members give generously of their time to attend up to three review meetings and comment on the final report. They are: David Belfall, Head of Housing and Area Regeneration Group, Scottish Executive; Richard Brown, Transition Team, Mayor and Assembly for London, Government Office for London; Peter Fullerton, Head, Urban and Rural Development, the National Assembly for Wales; Martin Gawith, Executive Director, Greater Nottingham Partnership; Coinneach Maclean, Scottish Business in the Community; Helen Macneil, Director, Glasgow Council for Voluntary Services; Shahid Malik, Chief Executive, Haringey Regeneration Agency; Gail Newton, Head of Policy, Scottish Homes; Michael Parkinson, Liverpool John Moores University; John Seargent, Policy and Research Director, Development Trust Association; and Richard Stubbs, Director, Newham On-line.

The research team is grateful to Scottish Homes for allowing us to build into this project the research results for the Scottish case studies, the bulk of which work had been commissioned by Scottish Homes. For this reason, the Scottish case studies were carried out about one year earlier than the English and Welsh case studies, although they have been updated wherever possible. Alison More and Jo Dean of the University of Glasgow, contributed to the Scottish case studies, and Alys Thomas, of the Business School, Glamorgan University, assisted with the Welsh Study.

Summary of key findings

This study reports on factors that influence the effectiveness of urban regeneration partnerships, and how they work within the emerging national policy context. Case studies were carried out in 27 partnerships in eight city-regions in England and Scotland and in the Welsh Valleys. In most of these, a 'cluster' of partnerships was examined: a regional or sub-regional partnership, a city-wide one and a local one. An Appendix describes the case studies and the key issues of partnership derived from their study.

In addition to factors of effectiveness, what are called 'foundation stones' of partnership were also examined. These influence the quality of partnership and the outcomes of regeneration, but are outside of the control of partnerships, except by lobbying. They are: the modernisation of local government, the regional development framework, and the need for a coordinated, effective national policy. The political agendas behind these issues are proceeding at a different pace in the three countries studied. The foundation stones are discussed in Section III.

Key lessons of partnership

The research team distilled information on factors that had a substantial influence on the effectiveness of partnership. The key lessons are as follows.

Leadership

Political and executive leadership are critical to the quality of partnership. In sub-regional and city-wide partnerships involving local government, as most do, the commitment of the council leader and the council's chief executive to

the objectives of the partnership is essential. Executive leadership at this spatial scale takes place either in, or with the support of, a strong chief executive's department of the lead local authority, or else it resides with motivated, paid staff of the partnership under an able director.

At all levels of partnership, strong, competent leadership by the chair of the partnership board, working closely with the director, heightens the visibility of the partnership, draws in reluctant partners and drives forward the regeneration agenda, thus ensuring that the partnership is more than a 'talking shop'.

Visioning and consensus building

Regeneration is a long-term task, requiring a 10- to 25-year horizon. Visioning processes, by whatever name, provide the opportunity for prospective partners to come together to develop a shared agenda for the future, to position the city-region in the economy, to enthuse residents, businesses and potential inward investors and to provide a broad benchmark of progress in the partnership. Visioning is often championed by the council leader.

Translation of vision into workable objectives

Vision statements must be carried through in a systematic manner to produce consensual, workable medium-term objectives, backed up by commitments to finance, human resources, targets and monitoring; or the vision will be discredited and the quality of partnership eroded.

Building community into partnership

Good partnerships with communities form around longer-term strategic development plans for the neighbourhood and the city rather than solely to secure regeneration funding. The best approaches integrate short-term participation exercises with improvements in local democracy, such as the advent of area forums in a number of local authorities. Formal agreements can help cement partnership, and demonstrate commitment of institutional partners to community groups let down in the past. Modest revenue funding for key community groups could bring real benefits in capacity building.

Drawing business into partnership

Business leaders are often drawn into partnership by a one-on-one approach from the leader of the council. They can make a valuable contribution to partnership, but have little patience with 'talking shops'. Partnership structure and operation will need to maximise the use of their time, with emphasis on vision and strategic development issues. Effective, sustained business involvement occurs when business representatives organise themselves before entering into partnership. This can be through an existing organisation, such as a chamber of commerce, or a regeneration-focused business partnership.

Inclusiveness versus efficiency

Partnerships suffer tension between the need to be inclusive as to partner organisations and the need for efficient, streamlined decision and management processes. Partnership boards must be kept to a reasonable number of formal members, with around 15 persons the norm on a main board. Other means to broaden the base of participation include a citizens' forum, a secondary operational board, and/or a core management team. Larger memberships require additional managerial resources to maintain enthusiasm and commitment.

In effective partnerships, Training and Enterprise Councils/Local Enterprise Councils, Chamber, educational organisations, the police and the health authority develop and manage key aspects of the regeneration strategy with other stakeholders, including community groups. This is important, because the longer the track record of practical mutual activity in the partnership, the easier partnership working becomes.

On nurturing partnership

This means paying attention to making the partnership work well. At the outset, or when partnership is weak, formal or informal attempts to build mutual understanding among partners can be undertaken. Leaders can build bridges with less enthusiastic partners, helping them overcome diffidence about partnership itself and to find benefits for their organisation in partnership working.

Human resources

Partnerships represent complex interpersonal and organisational interactions, so they are dependent on the quality of their people. Human aspects of partnership working – communication and diplomacy, building mutual understanding, learning that power sharing can increase agency effectiveness and so on – take time to learn. Confidence building is also important, particularly for board members – while they may be representatives of their organisations, they need to have the courage and mandate to take decisions and accept responsibilities on behalf of their agency in the partnership. Personal skills ought to be a key criterion in the selection of managers, staff and even board members.

For staffing of partnerships, although seconded staff can make a valuable contribution, full-time, paid staff, able to operate with a degree of independence from any partner, are better able to promote the partnership's strategic programme and to make effective use of its human and financial resources. It is also important to assist local councillors in partnership areas, the great majority now outside of local authority 'cabinets', to develop a productive role in ward representation and partnership, vis-à-vis local residents and the business community.

A culture of partnership

This is not only about success and failure in regeneration, determined by careful, constructive monitoring of outcomes and partnership quality, but also about underlying attitudes and values, reflected in working practices, which partners bring to the table. These are the elements of organisational culture, which can be altered to embrace partnership.

Partnerships can lose direction, or fall apart from public squabbling between partners who fail to develop a common agenda. Some are wound up, but this is seldom a viable option for visible, city-wide partnerships. Failure is not a crime, but the lessons of experience must be addressed in an honest manner and new, mutually agreeable ways of working set in place before a partnership is relaunched. Hearts and minds can be focused on the necessary steps through a relaunch.

Recommendations

Broadening the base of partnership

Effective partnerships are built on the involvement of key regional and local organisations. Thus, the active involvement is needed of health trusts, the Employment Service, the Benefits Agency and the police. Concerted effort also needs to be made to involve business in regeneration – only a minority of the partnerships studied had effective business involvement.

Genuinely empowering the community

A feature of too many regeneration areas is the feeling of residents that they have no influence over public decisions. They therefore lack confidence in public agencies as well as themselves. There is little recognition that community involvement ought to produce a transfer of power to those currently powerless. To work towards this, regeneration programmes should budget for community development and capacity building from the start, ensure that partners understand community development processes, enter into formal regeneration and service quality agreements or community plans, and measure success in terms of community confidence and skills, and residents' views of regeneration achievements.

Better local governance to aid regeneration

Many local councils are finding real benefit in supporting partnership with modernisation and new approaches to local democracy. Partners, from business to community, find that councils embracing modernisation are easier to work with

and make better, more committed, partners. To encourage innovation and foster transfer of best practice, each of the three countries studied, in their own way, would benefit from establishment of a government-sponsored, but partnership-organised, 'Modern Local Government Good Practice Unit', to help local authorities rethink and reposition their strategic and management role for the 21st century.

Joined-up action

Removing barriers to joined-up thinking means moving decision makers out of their organisational silos and making individuals, teams and whole agencies think differently about working practices and how this affects the fortunes of regeneration areas and disadvantaged households. Means to joined-up action to support partnership working include: corporate strategy approach in the local authority, coordinated regional development, and coordination and a changed organisational culture among central government departments. There is widespread concern among practitioners that central government departments fail to achieve a joined-up national policy framework.

A new financial regime

Effective regeneration requires an integrated approach to funding. Financial inflexibility within a plethora of new initiatives, often based on challenge funding with short time limits, may not deliver optimum benefits. The time is right for stakeholders to work together towards a more innovative approach to the funding of partnerships. The report suggests a contract with, and terms of reference for, partnership and bloc regeneration grants to local authorities.

Fostering a chain of sustainable development

Top-down and bottom-up integration is necessary to enhance regeneration at all levels – meaning positive linkage between neighbourhood, city, sub- and regional partnerships. This gives a chain of sustainable development *only as strong as its weakest link*. Political and funding structures should assist the establishment of partnerships at levels where they are needed but don't yet exist – some neighbourhood partnerships in adjacent local authorities, city-wide partnerships, which ought to exist in almost every city and town, and sub- and regional partnerships, the former around logical urban sub-regions or travel-to-work areas. Care should be taken to ensure that efforts are complementary so that, for example, Regional Development Agency-initiated partnerships do not undermine valuable, existing sub-regional partnerships.

Coherent regional framework

This is important for the support of partnership at all levels, by ensuring that economic development and inward investment directly underpin regeneration and social inclusion, providing a coherent land use framework – for example to ensure that out-of-town shopping or housing does not undermine inner-city vitality – and ensuring that development is not at the expense of the environment. These issues require a means for taking tough regional decisions; where they are avoided, partnership at lower spatial levels is less productive. In England, coordination between Government Offices for the Region, Regional Planning Guidance and RDA activity ought to provide an integrated framework for partnerships to work within. Scotland and Wales need to do more to develop a coherent regional development framework that provides a context for regeneration among single-tier local authorities.

A national urban policy

Central government should be promoting strategic urban development, to underpin regeneration, to balance spatial patterns of the country's economic development on a more equitable basis, and to support industrialised cities losing jobs and population. A national policy, linking urban and rural development and transport and investment in infrastructure, may be essential to allow partnerships, and the country as a whole, to achieve major objectives in the regeneration of our cities.

Are partnerships the key to Britain's urban regeneration?

In the past 10 years partnership has become a defining characteristic of British urban regeneration. This is in recognition of the fact that economic decline, social exclusion and area dereliction are problems that have proved too severe and complex to be resolved by any one agency, local government, business or community group acting alone.

The establishment of a partnership is also an essential step in securing central government regeneration funding. In England, the advent of the Single Regeneration Budget (SRB) Challenge Fund has seen a multiplication of local partnerships. There may be as many as 20 or 25 SRB projects in a local authority operating in parallel to related initiatives requiring partnership, such as City Pride, New Commitment to Regeneration, Education and Health Action Zones, New Deals for Community and Employment, Community Planning initiatives and other 'pathfinders' such as under the Best Value initiative.

Scottish programmes requiring a partnership approach include Social Inclusion Partnerships, New Housing Partnerships and Working for Communities Pathfinders. Partnership initiatives in Wales started more recently, since partnership was a not a firm requirement in the local authority directed Capital Challenge Fund. But Welsh funding programmes now requiring partnership include the Social Inclusion Fund and the People in Communities Programme. A partnership approach is also necessary to maximise funding opportunities under European programmes such as the European Regional Development Fund (ERDF); partnerships formed to prepare Single Programming Documents under Objective 1 status for the Welsh Valleys and South Yorkshire are examples. There will be similar partnerships for the new Objective 2 designation for areas suffering serious industrial decline.

As a result of these initiatives, in any one local authority area there may be 70 or 80 partnerships operating simultaneously. Activists and officials now speak of "partnership fatigue". Where partnerships are succeeding, they bring real added value to the regeneration task. Benefits include regeneration strategy suited to local requirements, real political commitment, avoidance of duplication of effort, policy coordination among agencies, joined-up action and encouragement of innovation. But where partnerships fail to work effectively, they can be a brake on regeneration and represent a lost opportunity in the face of pressing needs to end urban decline and social exclusion.

Challenges to regeneration partnerships

Despite many decades of regeneration activity in Britain, the task remains substantial. For example, recent research reveals that Britain's 20 major cities have lost half a million, mainly male, manufacturing jobs since 1981, a trend that shows little sign of abating (Turok and Edge, 1999). Loss of economic function and the economically able, mobile segments of the population from the former industrial cities has major impacts on service provision, such as education and health, for the residents remaining. As the client base declines, social problems become concentrated while the fixed costs of service delivery remain constant. In cities such as Glasgow or Manchester, where 60% of residents may live in designated regeneration areas, regeneration is not just an area-based, but a city-wide and regional, task.

Challenges to regeneration partnerships include:

- The need to achieve sustainability, or a long-term stream of benefits in regeneration, set against a history of regeneration initiatives, many of which have not achieved lasting benefit and have left people cynical about prospects.
- The need to derive economic and social renewal, and social inclusion, from the necessary but easier task of physical regeneration.
- The need to link national policy, regional and sub-regional governance, city-level strategy and local action in a coherent whole so that top-down and bottom-up initiatives are mutually supportive.
- The need to harness mainstream policy and services to regeneration requirements, given that more than 90% of public expenditure in regeneration areas is through mainstream budgets. Mainstream programmes then need to achieve better integration with the temporary, 'catalyst' funding streams that characterise regeneration programmes.
- The need to promote a potentially fruitful convergence of interests between the government's 'modernisation of local government' agenda and regeneration. Within the modernisation agenda, an important task is to develop local democracy and neighbourhood initiatives to balance a mainly top-down approach in area regeneration often accompanied by problematic or tokenistic participation exercises.

There has been much useful analysis lately of urban problems, including by the Urban Task Force, the Social Exclusion Unit, the Scottish Social Exclusion Network, and leading up to a new Urban White Paper for England and Wales (Urban Task Force, 1999; Scottish Social Inclusion Network, 1999; SEU, 1998). But more of this analysis has focused on what we ought to do, and rather less on the equally important question of how we are going to do it. This distinction mirrors the important relationship between regeneration strategy and partnership, *the what to do* and *the how to do it*. Certainly, strategy derived in the absence of a partnership, however logical and intelligent, is likely to be largely ignored by key stakeholders, because they have not had a hand in fashioning it and thus have no sense of ownership. But 'talking shop' partnerships which are not grappling with real

strategic issues waste partners' valuable time and financial resources and bring the partnership approach into disrepute. The quality of regeneration strategy and the quality of partnership are intimately related.

Effectiveness in partnership

Despite continuing challenges of regeneration and a veritable explosion in numbers of partnerships, little is known about why some partnerships are effective and others are not. Many *are* succeeding in terms of meeting their aims and objectives, including some partnerships documented here. In these cases, partnership is a useful and rewarding way to tackle regeneration. But for every successful partnership there are others that have achieved little or nothing.

The purpose of the research on which this report is based has been to identify the key lessons of partnership, and critical issues about partnership and local governance which may affect the future of cities and urban communities. The intention is to inspire improved partnerships in future, and to foster adjustments in urban policy to support local action.

The method of inquiry

Case studies were carried out in England, Wales and Scotland – in nine 'nested clusters' of 27 partnerships. These are described briefly at the end of this chapter, and in detail in the Appendix. For the most part, regional or sub-regional and city-wide partnerships were studied, and they also provide the context for a selected neighbourhood or estate-based initiative. In a few cities without sub-regional partnership, a city-wide partnership is studied with two area/neighbourhood or thematic partnerships.

For each partnership cluster, around 30-35 one- to two-hour interviews were carried out with key players in the partnership and within the relevant structure of local governance. (The term 'local governance' is used in this report to mean the influences on urban development not only of local government but of the other organisations and community groups that are in a position to 'sway' the development process. *The Oxford Dictionary* uses the term 'sway' in its definition of governance.) Discussions in 'focus' groups were also organised with: residents in the local partnership area, with community activists, and with a cross-section of local government officials concerned with area regeneration.

Assessment criteria

Assessing partnership is not the most straightforward of tasks. There are difficulties in assessing the relationship between the quality of a partnership and the outcomes of that partnership, and difficulties in understanding the relationship between partnership operation and the competence and commitment of partner organisations.

On the outcome side, it is often difficult to make an assessment on how well a partnership is operating on the basis of what should be the most straightforward outcome measure, the achievement of tangible regeneration. This is because achievement is influenced not only by the quality of partnership, but by:

- The base case, including the industrial and social history of an area, the effects of migration of residents, sometimes called 'population churn', and residualisation of households with low educational attainment, poor employment prospects and/or social problems in neighbourhoods and cities as a whole.
- The influence of different styles of local governance over many years.
- Current, powerful economic factors, influenced by the global economy, which result in closure of local industrial plants and whole sectors of a local economy, with attendant job losses.

On the organisational side, the quality of a partnership is substantially influenced not only by factors that define the partnership itself, but also by factors that define the quality of governance and management of the constituent partner organisations, or *stakeholders*. This is particularly true of local government as an influential lead agency in many partnerships. A poorly managed organisation is unlikely to be a useful regeneration partner. But conversely, a well managed organisation may be a poor partner if its strategic objectives are not reflected in partnership objectives.

To get around these difficulties, the research team developed a preliminary *partnership evaluation framework*, based in the first instance on our

many previous research projects on regeneration and refined as a result of this research (see, for example, Carley and Kirk, 1998, 1999; Dean et al, 1999). In each partnership, therefore, we have looked for a variety of factors that appear relevant to success or failure, including:

- the role of political and executive *leadership* in fostering the partnership;
- use of *visioning* processes and *consensus building* towards regeneration strategy;
- translation of vision into practical, *workable objectives* to be monitored over time;
- the breadth of *membership* of the partnership;
- various methods of partnership *operation*;
- the role of *human resources* and personal aptitude for partnership;
- the development of an *organisational culture* which rewards partnership working.

As will be seen from the following chapters, each of these factors is underpinned by an additional set of sub-factors. The complexity of the framework reflects the nature of the partnerships themselves – complex organisational arrangements as well as dynamic entities which can change dramatically in a short time. Further 'nested', mutually influencing, sub-regional, city and local partnerships present additional organisational, political and managerial challenges. The purpose of this research is to grapple with this complexity in order to *simplify and highlight key factors* that can be influenced to improve the quality of partnership.

Beyond this, this report identifies and clarifies the importance of some 'foundation stones' of effective regeneration partnerships. These are generally outside the control of partnerships (except by lobbying), but condition the vitality of partnership and the success of regeneration. They are:

- the agenda of local government modernisation;
- the need for a workable, evolving framework of regional development and governance;
- the coherence and supportive nature of central government policy.

In England, Wales and Scotland, each of these agendas is evolving at a different pace and with different institutional structures. This is due to varying approaches of the Welsh and Scottish Offices (now Scottish Executive and National Assembly for Wales) and the Department of the

Figure 1: An enabling framework for partnership in urban regeneration

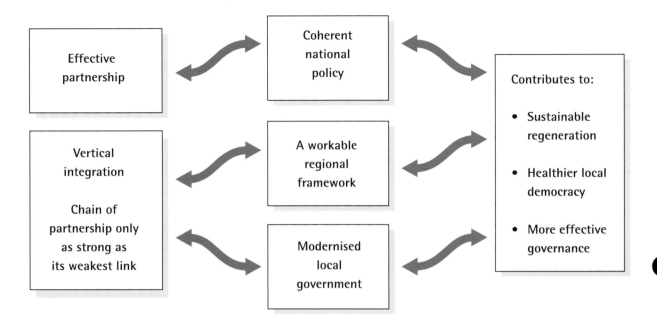

Environment, Transport and the Regions (DETR), different outcomes of the most recent local government reorganisation and, of course, the advent of the Scottish and Welsh Parliaments. We have attempted to highlight some differences in key issues as they affect regeneration partnerships. However, because of the complexity of what are rapidly evolving agendas, definitive statements or closely linked comparisons have not been attempted.

Organisation of the report

The above factors feature in the organisation of the report, which is set out in Figure 1. The report is in three sections, Sections II and III following this introductory chapter.

Section II describes generic lessons on improving the quality of partnerships. Section III focuses on the foundation stones of partnership listed above. Conclusions and recommendations follow. An Appendix describes the nine case study clusters of partnerships and the key lessons to emerge from the analysis of those partnerships. Figure 2 sets out a typology of the partnerships studied, which are summarised below.

Summary of the case studies

East London – Newham

The research looked at: the Thames Gateway Partnership, founded in 1995 to develop strategic vision for East London, north and south of the Thames, as an economic and social region, and linking 12 local authorities; the Newham Chief Executive's Forum, which brings together representatives of key agencies; and, at the local level, the SRB-funded Forest Gate and Plaistow Sustainable Communities Initiative. The 10-year-old East London Partnership of business organisations was also studied.

Greater Manchester

As a key example of a sub-regional partnership, City Pride forms the top level of the case study. The study also included the Salford Partnership, formed in 1995, a local authority-wide partnership with a thematic focus, which also acts as an umbrella for area regeneration schemes. It is a 'pathfinder' under the New Commitment to Regeneration initiative. At the local level is the Cheetham and Broughton Partnership, a joint initiative of Manchester and Salford City Councils as part of SRB 2. This was the first two-council

SRB. The partnership is an attempt at joint working between two councils with different cultures and approaches. Its importance lies in the fact that there are likely to be more regeneration areas that straddle administrative boundaries.

Birmingham

Birmingham City Pride is a long-standing, city-wide partnership with responsibility for the development and monitoring of a strategic vision for the city. The Birmingham Economic Development Partnership is a multi-agency delivery partnership focused specifically on the economy. At the neighbourhood level, the research examined the Handsworth Community Safety Project, part of a SRB 4 scheme, Community Safety in Birmingham.

Tees Valley – Middlesbrough

The study examined three partnerships: the Tees Valley Joint Strategy Unit (TVJSU), a joint local authority partnership for sub-regional planning and strategic development across five local authorities; Middlesbrough Direct, a new city-wide partnership; and, at the local level, Grove Hill 2000, an area regeneration partnership.

South Yorkshire – Sheffield

Research focused on the South Yorkshire Forum, a sub-regional partnership responsible for drafting the Objective 1 Single Programming Document (SPD); the city-wide partnership Sheffield First; and, locally, the Netherthorpe and Upperthorpe Community Alliance, an SRB 1 area. Evolving partnership approaches at a regional level were also studied, including the Yorkshire and Humberside Assembly and Chamber and 'Yorkshire Forward', the new Regional Development Area (RDA).

The Welsh Valleys – Rhondda Cynon Taff

The study looked at the Valleys Partnership, a regional partnership covering the Valleys Objective 1 area of nine local authorities. The partnership has 'regional facilitators' appointed from two local authorities, and a broad membership. Within this context, regeneration activity was studied in the local authority Rhondda Cynon Taff, and local regeneration by a community development trust in the village of Ferndale, whose pit closed in 1959.

Glasgow

The Glasgow Alliance, first formally established in 1993, is the key city-wide partnership. Relaunched in 1998, its initial focus on area regeneration has widened to a city development remit. The Gorbals Regeneration Partnership is a mainly public sector alliance, formed in 1986 to oversee the development of this historically deprived area. It was constituted as a Social Inclusion Partnership (SIP) in 1999. The Crown Street Regeneration Project dates from 1990 and is a vehicle for delivering the wholesale redevelopment of one neighbourhood, involving public sector agencies working with community representatives.

Lanarkshire

The Lanarkshire Alliance links two local authorities established with the reorganisation of local government in Scotland, that is, North Lanarkshire Council and South Lanarkshire Council, in a strategic regional partnership involving the Lanarkshire Development Agency, Scottish Homes and the Lanarkshire Health Board. The North Lanarkshire Partnership operates strategic partnerships across the local authority area. At a local level, the Motherwell North SIP is concerned with the regeneration of four disadvantaged areas in Motherwell.

Edinburgh

The Edinburgh Capital City Partnership (CCP) is a city-wide initiative coordinating area regeneration and social inclusion within the local authority boundary. It was established in 1995 in response to the government regeneration Programme for Partnership. North Edinburgh Area Renewal Partnership (NEAR) was launched in 1993 independently of any government funding programmes, although it is now a SIP. NEAR has a comprehensive regeneration agenda for this large area of public sector housing. Within the NEAR area, the Pilton Partnership, a long-standing, staffed community organisation, is focused primarily on community development and poverty issues. It is formally and informally linked both to NEAR and to CCP.

Figure 2: A typology of the case study approach

Geographical focus	Large complex*	Smaller focused†
Regional/ Sub-regional	England	
	Thames Gateway Partnership, East London City Pride, Manchester The Tees Valley Joint Strategy Unit South Yorkshire Forum	
	Scotland	
	The Lanarkshire Alliance	
	Wales	
	The Valleys Partnership, South Wales	
City-wide or local authority	England	
	Chief Executive's Forum, Newham, East London The Salford Partnership City Pride, Birmingham	Birmingham Economic Development Partnership
	Middlesbrough Direct Sheffield First	
	Scotland	
	The Glasgow Alliance Edinburgh Capital City Partnership The North Lanarkshire Partnership	
	Wales	
	Rhonnda Cynon Taff, South Wales	
Area or neighbourhood	England	
	Forest Gate and PLaistow Sustainable Communities Initiative Cheetham and Broughton Partnership, Greater Manchester	Handsworth Community Safety Project, Birmingham
	Grove Hill 2000, Middlesbrough Netherthorpe and Upperthorpe Community Alliance, Sheffield	
	Scotland	
	The Gorbals Regeneration Partnership‡, Glasgow	Crown Street Regeneration Project, Glasgow
	North Edinburgh Area Renewal Priority Partnership Area§ Motherwell North Priority Partnership Area§	The Pilton Partnership, Edinburgh
	Wales	
		Ferndale Arts Factory Community Development Trust

Notes: * Defined as involving partners from a broad range of agencies and across the public, private and third sectors around a comprehensive regeneration or development agenda.
† Defined as partnerships involving a smaller range of players, sometimes from a single sector, around a more tightly defined regeneration or development agenda.
‡ Since the fieldwork for this research was undertaken, this has been reconstituted as the Gorbals Social Inclusion Partnership and has been sustantially restructured.
§ Since the fieldwork for this research was undertaken, both the NEAR and North Motherwell partnerships have been renamed as Social Inclusion Partnerships rather than Priority Partnership Areas.

Section II: Building strong partnerships

2

The lessons of partnership

Figure 3: Lessons of effective partnership

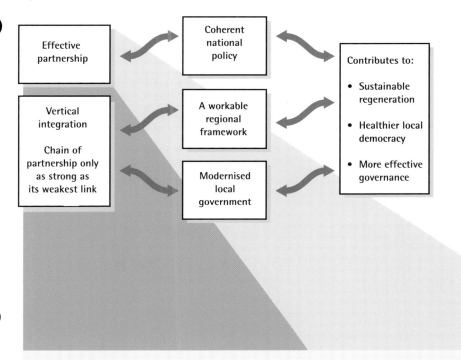

Key points

- Strong political and executive leadership at most senior level

- Use of visioning processes as a focal point for consensus building among partners

- Translation of vision into political objectives for urban development and local regeneration

- Inclusion of key stakeholders in partnership: community, business, police, health authority, education sector and others

- Effective partnership structure – a balance between inclusiveness and effectiveness

- High quality human resources as the backbone of partnership

- Organisational culture supportive of partnership

The importance of political leadership

Strong leadership plays a vital role in partnership success. Leadership is important for:

- bringing visibility to a partnership;
- providing evidence of commitment at a senior level;
- cementing partnership, by diplomatically drawing in reluctant partners;
- driving forward a sometime contentious regeneration agenda;
- encouraging genuine financial and human resource commitment to the achievement of that agenda;
- promoting shared ownership of the process.

Partnership depends on both *political* and *managerial* leadership.

In sub-regional and city-wide partnerships in which local government is the lead agency, the quality of involvement and commitment of council leaders and councils' chief executives can make or break partnership. At all levels of partnership, strong, able leadership by the chair of the partnership board, frequently working closely with a paid director or chief executive of the partnership, plays a key role in driving forward the regeneration agenda, ensuring the partnership is more than a 'talking shop'.

Sub-regional partnerships require a political legitimacy which can be conferred only by the leaders of their respective councils, most often by their personal involvement. Successful city-wide and sub-regional partnerships almost always have this commitment from the council leader and chief executive, which is usually a prerequisite for drawing in other partners at a 'chief executive' level. Although senior involvement does not guarantee a culture of partnership, this is unlikely to develop without their commitment.

The role of leadership is apparent in East London's many partnerships. For example, board meetings of the Thames Gateway Partnership, which represents 12 local authorities, regularly attract seven or eight council leaders. Participation at the leader level is seen as essential for this multi-local authority partnership to function and to address the strategic challenges that are at the heart of the regeneration task facing East London.

At the local authority level, in the London Borough of Newham the leader has launched the visionary Newham 2010 initiative, which is the council "listening to its citizens" over future aspirations, perceptions on council services, Best Value and democratic participation. The first meeting attracted 500 community representatives. Within this context, the Chief Executive's Forum, chaired personally by the local authority's Chief Executive, legitimates active, committed involvement of other institutional partners, including the Metropolitan Police at the borough superintendent level, and the East London and the City Health Authority at the deputy chief executive level. They in turn provide strong leadership on regeneration and partnership within their own organisations, guaranteeing a real commitment to the regeneration strategy and to joint working over issues.

Getting the balance right between effective leadership capable of driving partnership forward, and yet developing a shared sense of ownership of the process among partners, has been a key challenge faced by the Salford Partnership. In Salford's New Commitment Pathfinder, strong political commitment to the partnership from the leader and deputy leader of the council, together with the fact that the partnership is run from the Chief Executive's Department, have been effective in driving the partnership. Most partners report they are largely comfortable having the city in the driving seat, although there has been growing pressure recently to make the process feel like more of a mutual endeavour. This is being tackled, through different partners taking the lead on specific regeneration programmes, rotating the venue of meetings between partners, and, crucially, placing an emphasis on facilitating debate and discussion between partners in order to make best use of their potential inputs.

Lack of leadership will stifle partnership action. Until its relaunch in 1998, the Glasgow Alliance suffered from a lack of clarity over leadership, with local politicians unwilling to take on a leadership role and the chair of the partnership rotating among partners in a lacklustre fashion. However, the profile of the Alliance was raised quickly when a new leader of Glasgow Council took on the mantle of champion of the partnership, raising its profile in the city and the Scottish Office. This initiative dovetailed with Scottish Office support (financial and otherwise) for a review of the Alliance, and these two forces helped generate significant new momentum.

Executive leadership

> Political and executive leadership go hand-in-hand. Executive leadership of many successful sub-regional and city-wide partnerships takes place either in, or with the support of, a strong chief executive's department of the lead local authority. In other cases it resides with motivated, paid staff of the partnership under an able chief executive.

In addition to political support, successful partnerships require strong managerial leadership. In some city-wide and sub-regional partnerships, as in Newham and Manchester, the Chief Executive's Department can play a vital role in driving forward the agenda of partnership. In other cases, paid and seconded staff, almost always under a paid chief executive of the regeneration partnership, provide that leadership. Not surprisingly, partnerships without strong, clear leadership, or those that try to 'get by' with busy staff seconded on a part-time basis from the local authority, are less successful.

Managerial leadership can be shared. Manchester City Pride and Manchester Council's regeneration programmes benefit not only from full commitment of the chief executive to partnership, but from a major time commitment to regeneration of two assistant chief executives who have a keen interest in both strategic and local regeneration issues. They can speak for the Council as a whole and, when necessary, 'knock heads together' between line departments to promote a coherent approach of the local authority. The Council's expressed aspiration is that every senior council official will feel confident to speak for the Council as whole when interacting with residents rather than only on behalf of more narrow departmental interests. Similarly, in Middlesbrough, the Council has reorganised itself so that four corporate directors answer to the chief executive, one of whom has direct responsibility for the city-wide partnership, Middlesbrough Direct.

Newham's Regeneration and Partnerships Division (RPD) of the Chief Executive's Department has 30 staff, under a director who reports directly to the chief executive. RPD develops the Council's overall regeneration strategy, prepared by thematic groups linking council officers to external partners, in the context of a wider Newham 2010 initiative. RPD also manages major programmes for area regeneration, anti-poverty and welfare rights. Their work is overseen politically by a Regeneration Board of councillors, and they liase to other departments through the Regeneration Strategy Officer Group. Each partnership in the borough has a designated staff member who together link local partnerships at borough level. Staff members also carry out generic regeneration functions, such as securing European funding. The RPD also acts as a secretariat to the Chief Executive's Forum. The benefits of this strong managerial leadership are obvious in the borough's regeneration achievements and in a very positive view of partnership processes taken by non-local authority partners.

Executive leadership can also deliver real benefits in neighbourhood partnership, and needn't always come from the local authority. Glasgow's Crown Street Regeneration Project has benefited from a clear lead from the Glasgow Development Agency (GDA), the local enterprise company. The organisation's chief executive has acted in a champion role, helping secure and maintain the involvement of senior players from the other main public sector investors in the project, particularly the local authority (at member and officer level) and Scottish Homes. This has been essential to secure the bending of mainstream capital budgets of the GDA and Scottish Homes towards delivering an ambitious master plan for the area, as well as the investment of the City Council in road realignment and in a training and employment initiative.

Visioning and consensus building

> Regeneration is invariably a long-term task, requiring a 10- to 25-year horizon. Visioning processes, by whatever name, provide the opportunity for prospective partners to come together to develop a shared agenda for the future, to enthuse residents, businesses and potential inward investors and provide a broad benchmark of progress in the partnership.

In sub-regional and city-wide partnerships, visioning is frequently taken forward by the leader or leaders of the appropriate local authorities, as in Newham 2020 reported above, although other agencies, such as Scottish Homes for the Edinburgh Capital City Partnership, can also 'get the ball rolling' in visioning. At the neighbourhood/estate level, residents' groups often take the lead, organising 'community planning weekends' and other events, sometimes with specialist help. Visioning helps the partnership determine the general thrust of regeneration, but, perhaps most importantly, provides the first round of development of the *shared agenda* without which genuine partnership will not emerge.

Linking vision to community participation in strategic regeneration, the Thames Gateway Partnership (TGP) in association with the Community Network organised a Community Vision Conference. Community Network, organised by TGP, links 373 community and voluntary groups across East London. The Conference, attracting 200 delegates, addressed strategic regeneration issues and the quality of community participation and network development in a session called 'Mere gesture or genuine partnership?'. It then went on to look at: representation and accountability, environment and quality of life, skills, transport, manufacturing, tourism and community safety. The resultant report, *A community vision for the Thames Gateway London*, identifies the following key issues for taking forward: capacity building in the Community Network, linkage between regional, strategic development and local aspirations, and linkage between short-term programmes and long-term strategy.

In Wales, the Valleys Partnership has worked hard to generate a Single Programming Document to fulfil the requirements of its Objective 1 status. However a 'Valleys-wide' vision is said to be lacking. The current relatively weak partnership arrangement is led by officer representatives of neighbouring single-tier local authorities, who are not in the political or organisational position to generate the high-level vision that may be essential for regional development in an area hard hit by deindustrialisation. As in Scotland, the last round of local government reorganisation left a legacy of relatively small unitary authorities with no regional planning superstructure of the type provided by Government Offices and Regional Planning Guidance in England. Without a strong sense of vision for the Valleys, it may be difficult for the Valleys Partnership to lure inward investment away from the booming M4 corridor, or to mediate between incompatible visions for the Valleys, such as between industry and tourism. This point is taken up in the next chapter.

Translation of vision into workable objectives

Visioning must lead to more specific objectives and targets. A consensus-building vision is a good first step – but it is almost never sufficient to cement partnership and move forward regeneration strategy. In the past, vision processes were often discredited because they didn't go beyond the 'motherhood and apple pie' stage to link visions to workable objectives.

Vision statements must be carried through in a systematic manner to produce consensual, workable medium and short-term objectives, backed up by commitments to finance, human resources, targets of achievement and monitoring systems; otherwise the vision will be discredited and the quality of partnership eroded.

Too few partnerships clearly articulate objectives in this manner. Nor is it sufficient for the strategy to simply be a list of what is already being done separately by partners – the whole purpose of the partnership must be to generate and be able to measure value-added or 'multiplier effects' which come from coordinated action and resource expenditure among partners. Being as specific as possible about partnership objectives will pay dividends during implementation, accepting that objectives and targets can, and will, evolve as circumstances change.

The strategy of the Glasgow Alliance, *Creating Tomorrow's Glasgow*, sets out a range of measures for identifying progress. For example, headline targets for key issues are set, with time-scales attached, such as: 'Reduce the current amount of long-term derelict land by 50% in five years'. In the first instance, programme monitoring will be done by using partners' pre-existing monitoring and evaluation systems. However, there is a recognition that new integrated information systems are required, capable of measuring linkages and interactions between programmes, in order to measure the cumulative effect of the partnership. In the Strategy, the Alliance also suggests the need for more qualitative assessment of progress, based on the views of the city's residents. Mechanisms such as surveys and a citizens' panel are planned in order to establish a current baseline of resident views and the nature of improvements achieved by the year 2003.

A problem with city-wide strategies can be a lack of 'connectivity' to the interests of the wider community. To overcome this, a key feature of the work of Birmingham City Pride is to work out the 'dynamics' of their strategy and establish a route to realise that vision. Part of this process involves monitoring progress on key objectives through a set of 'quality of life indicators' which ought to be relevant to the needs of all citizens. Public consultation is undertaken over regular reports on progress. The Partnership takes very seriously its 'duty of scrutiny' over the actions (or lack thereof) of partners – including of the local authority. City Pride can and will publicly challenge key delivery agencies, such as the City's Housing Department, on their performance against the Partnership's stated strategic objectives.

Making vision work also involves the development of institutional capacity. In Greater Manchester the City Pride process, although with a consensual vision, has not always provided an arena in which to reconcile practical differences between partners or negotiate between their competing priorities. For example, SRB bids are still generated separately by each authority, and there has been little in the way of cooperation between the four partner authorities aimed at maximising the possibility of success. This suggests that past relationships between the partner local authorities were not yet developed sufficiently for the partnership to survive difficult compromises. However, the partnership may be on the brink of developing such capacity. For example, through City Pride, a 'managing partnership' for disbursing ESF Objective 2 funds has been established, which makes difficult decisions about relative priorities for investment in the constituent local authorities. Other vital inter-local authority projects nurtured by City Pride include Marketing Manchester, and a new coordinating inward investment agency.

Including key stakeholders in partnership

Many public sector partners come readily to the roundtable of partnership, albeit with varying degrees of commitment. More problematic are attempts to find a way to genuinely involve local residents in both strategic and neighbourhood partnerships. It can also be difficult for partnerships to attract representatives of the business community; business involvement in the

partnerships studied here ranged from a high level of involvement in a few cases to nil involvement in others.

Building community representation into partnership

For many partnerships, achieving meaningful 'community involvement' is difficult. For institutional partners, there is confusion about the difference between community and neighbourhood groups and their role in partnership, and voluntary organisations, the latter of which may also be service providers. Although commitment to community involvement is expressed, again and again, for institutional partners, the extent and timing of community involvement was said to be of concern in that, if "expectations are raised" before funding is secured, political problems arise. There is always concern that community participation can mean participation by a small number of dedicated activists with the time and inclination to attend the many meetings necessary to get partnerships off the ground.

There is confusion over different aspects of community participation, including the following:

- *Consultation:* which is securing the views of residents of a regeneration area, for example by surveys, panels and juries.
- *Representation:* of community members on regeneration partnerships, including board membership.
- *Service involvement:* in decision making about local service priorities and assessment of the quality of service delivery.
- *Empowerment:* where community and neighbourhood groups take their own decisions and control resources, for example, through development trusts or community-based housing associations[1].

Given some clarity over the different types of participation, an early step in partnership formation should be the assessment (or self-assessment) of local community capacity, which can vary substantially from one community to the next. There is real evidence from the local case studies, for example of the involvement of the

---

[1] We are grateful to David Belfall of the Scottish Executive for suggesting these distinctions.

Pilton Partnership in North Edinburgh Area Renewal, that community capacity can grow steadily and substantially through involvement in a regeneration partnership programme.

From the community side, many groups still feel that 'purse holders' and information hoarding agencies dictate the terms and conditions of partnership. There is "as yet to be any sense of equality"; "the local authority invites participation and then takes over", "presenting decisions already taken for rubber-stamping". There are said to be too many energy-sapping participation exercises, not formally linked to subsequent action programmes that benefit the community. Where funding is scarce, community groups find that, rather than engaging in partnership with each other as equals, they are forced to be like "dogs squabbling over a bone", over small amounts of funds. The short-term nature of funding undermines the long-term task of community development. Community representatives also resent an 'organisational culture' of partnership, in which it is assumed that partnership processes should be dominated by the norms and values of paid professionals rather than by the needs and aspirations of residents.

Despite such concerns, the research found many inspiring examples of community initiative, from the 10-year-old Community Links in Newham to the Arts Factory in Rhondda. The latter, a community development trust, is a 10-year-old partnership which takes an holistic view on regeneration, taps into community strengths, draws resources into the community and lobbies government. To get around unstable funding, it has developed a community business approach, including a landscaping company, a garden centre, an environmental arts consultancy, a pottery workshop, a computer-aided graphic design service and a property maintenance service. The Arts Factory employs 28 local residents and secures 45% of its revenue from trade and training contracts.

But even the most sophisticated community initiatives in high-quality partnerships feel that more effort is required to ensure that local communities and residents are empowered partners in regeneration. There is also lack of opportunity for local activists to be involved in strategic partnership at the city-wide or sub-regional level, thus integrating neighbourhood initiative with strategic levels of action. Edinburgh is unusual in that community

representatives from the local partnership areas sit as directors on the board of the city-wide strategic partnership and have played a central role in its development. This level of involvement has been facilitated by the fact that local community organisations are well resourced and supported by dedicated staff. The CCP involves experienced activists who have built up strong relationships with key officers, while maintaining a critical edge to their role in partnership. Other positive exceptions include Newham, where a key organisation, Community Links, sits on the Chief Executive's Forum and there are innovative forms of participation including street forums and 'walk-about neighbourhood analyses' by local residents in combination with officials; and Birmingham, where community, ethnic minority and young people's representatives are integrated into the City Pride structure.

Just as involving community groups generally requires real effort, so partnerships also need to make extra effort to ensure that ethnic minority residents have meaningful involvement in partnership structures. For example, over 50% of Britain's residents from ethnic minority backgrounds live in London, so it not surprising that East London partnerships make additional effort in this regard. In Newham minority residents take part in partnership in three ways: first through direct representation, such as through the Newham Council for Racial Equality sitting on the Community Safety partnership chaired by the Metropolitan Police; second, through participation in partnerships for areas, such as the Green Street SRB, which has a high proportion of residents and traders from ethnic minority backgrounds. Third, and most important, is the increasing involvement of residents from ethnic minority backgrounds in mainstream politics, such as Newham's 23 local authority councillors from Afro-Caribbean and Asian backgrounds – through employment, for example, as local government officers; or by their working through, and managing, community organisations, for example Apna Ghar – a self-help group for Asian women working through Newham's Community Links organisation.

Drawing business into partnership

Given that market failure is a symptom of urban decline, and that lack of employment opportunity is a major factor in social exclusion, business involvement in partnership ought to be a high priority. But drawing business into partnership can be difficult. Three partnership areas studied in this research were relatively successful in this regard: East London, Birmingham and Manchester. Others had less success – ranging from patchy business involvement to none at all. The three cases of achievement all represent 10 years or more of serious effort to secure business involvement in partnership.

Four points are relevant. First, business leaders tend to be highly directed individuals who guard their limited time resources carefully. Any partnership that appears to be a 'talking shop' will quickly lose the interest of business representatives.

Second, business leaders at the chief executive level are seldom interested in discussion about the operational or detailed expenditure aspects of regeneration programmes, preferring to donate time to genuine strategic development issues. Successful partnerships recognise this, sometimes creating opportunities for strategic and operational levels of participation. A good example is the East London Partnership (ELP), which is separate from but complementary to the other partnerships studied in East London. ELP links 37 East London and City blue-chip and medium-sized firms and business leaders to local authority partnerships and neighbourhood projects. ELP focuses on strategic regeneration through a main board, concerned with East London as a whole, and on area regeneration through area boards and secondments of business staff to community projects. ELP has a small, paid secretariat. Although the Partnership has hitherto worked at the three borough levels of Newham, Tower Hamlets and Hackney, it is now establishing links to the Thames Gateway Partnership and initiating an East London Business Alliance, chaired by the Chair of Ford UK.

ELP is a business partnership which, having first clearly defined its own interests in East London's development and the way it wants to work, then reaches out to broader partnerships to offer assistance in strategic advice, cash donations and by secondment of business personnel to community groups. Local groups, such as Newham's Community Links, rate its assistance highly. ELP, having a clear vision and an efficient way of working, gets maximum benefit from the donated time of busy chief executives. The role of a small dedicated staff, funded entirely by the business partners, is vital in ensuring that ELP works to maximum effectiveness.

Third, business participation in partnership can be accessed through a number of different channels. One is for council leaders and others to approach business leaders on an individual basis, to draw them into partnership. This has proved to be a successful approach in Manchester partnerships, including Hulme, and now for the new East Manchester regeneration company. Another approach to business involvement is through a separate business partnership, as in East London, or through the Chamber of Commerce, as in Birmingham. Birmingham Economic Development Partnership (BEDP) includes the City Council, Chamber of Commerce and Industry, and Birmingham and Solihull TEC. In 1998 the partners produced an Economic Development Strategy representing their shared vision. The preparatory review involved senior management and had full backing of partners. At that stage, there was a feeling that the time was right to integrate services offered by the three partners to remove confusion and duplication. The partnership has agreed that, to improve service delivery, staff could be 'co-located' to the agency with lead responsibility. The notion of co-location represents a fundamental shift in working practice and partnership, moving away from an individual agency approach to service delivery to a more integrated mode.

Fourth, from the point of view of non-business partners, there is often a mistaken assumption that securing TEC or LEC involvement is the same as business involvement. Most people in business view these organisations as quasi-public agencies, not necessarily speaking for the private sector.

Senior business leaders are often drawn into partnership by a one-on-one approach from the leader of the council. They can make a valuable contribution to partnership, but they have little patience with 'talking shops'. Partnership structure and operation will need to maximise use of their time, with emphasis on both vision and practical strategic development issues.

Successful, sustained business involvement in partnership, over 10 years or more, occurs when business representatives organise themselves before entering into partnership. This can be accomplished through an existing business organisation, such as the Chamber of Commerce in Birmingham, or a regeneration-driven business partnership, such as the East London Partnership.

Other partners in regeneration

One of the positive findings of the research is the extent to which, in successful partnerships, other important players have been drawn not only around the partnership table, but into the development of regeneration strategy and objectives. These include the TECs/LECs, higher and further education organisations and universities, the police, the Employment Service and health authorities and trusts.

In effective partnerships, partners such as TECs/LECs, educational organisations, the police and the health authority develop and manage key aspects of the regeneration strategy in association with other stakeholders including community groups. This is important because, the longer the track record of reasonably successful mutual activity in the partnership, the easier partnership working becomes.

In Newham, partners sitting on the Chief Executive's Forum themselves organise partnerships around specific issues such as community safety and health, making use of network contacts that the forum provides. For example, the Community Safety Steering Group is chaired by a divisional commander of the Metropolitan Police and includes the Council's chief executive, the director of social services, a chief probation officer, chief executive of the Chamber of Commerce and the chief executive of the Newham Council for Racial Equality. Another key organisation is the University of East London, with active involvement in both partnership and strategic development. The latter includes a new campus in Docklands adjacent to City Airport, with a Thames Gateway Technology Centre to promote employability and business start-up in the sub-region and, more generally, 'learning-led regeneration'. The East London and City Health Authority is also active in many partnerships including an Health Action Zone and many SRB partnerships. Other partnership initiatives include Newham On-Line, for easy Internet access for local people to service information, and a Centre for Innovation and Partnerships, of the Newham College of Further Education.

In Birmingham, too, community safety is being addressed at both the city-wide and local levels. Previous partnership activity included joint working with police, the City Council and the Probation Service but the impact was limited. However, the 1998 Crime and Disorder Act meant

the establishment of the Birmingham Community Safety Partnership, which at the strategic level links the chief executive of the Council and the Assistant Chief Constable of West Midlands. At first the partnership experienced difficulty due to differing management cultures. But joint undertaking of a crime audit helped to bring partners together and strengthen mutual trust.

Perhaps the only exception to this record of stakeholder involvement is that, although education authorities sit on some partnership boards, there is only infrequent involvement of primary and secondary students. They ought to play a role in regeneration, particularly in visioning how they want their future environment to look – within the course of a single 10-year regeneration programme, many of these young people will have become the young adults of tomorrow; they will be either part of the problem, or part of the solution. Middlesbrough's proposed Youth Parliament, as part of its city-wide partnership, may be one way of involving young people in vision and regeneration.

Inclusiveness versus effectiveness? Effective structure of partnership

Many partnerships suffer tension between the need to be inclusive as to partner organisations and the need for effective, streamlined decision and management processes. Partnership boards must be kept to a reasonable number of formal members, with experience suggesting no more than around 15 persons on the main board. Other means to broaden the base of participation, such as a citizens' forum, and sub-board structures, such as a secondary or day-to-day operational board, or a core management team, may be needed. Larger partnership membership requires additional managerial resources to maintain enthusiasm and commitment.

There are many options for formal partnership structures, organisationally and legally, but little indication that one is preferable to another. More important is a participatory process for key stakeholders to be involved in developing clear, fair and manageable partnership arrangements so that they have their full backing and reflect local organisational culture and requirements. These arrangements can be formalised in a code of practice to which all partners sign up. The opposite of this is a partnership structure determined in advance by the lead agency – often in the past, the local authority – which is unsuitable or disagreeable to other stakeholders, weakening their commitment to the partnership.

Whatever the original structure, most partnerships find they need to reorganise at some point in their lives around issues of inclusiveness and effectiveness. Sometimes this is accomplished by:

- Establishing a main, or strategic, partnership board for consideration of strategic development issues for the city or the region, and a subsidiary or sub-board structure, such as an operational board, which oversees the specific requirements of regeneration programmes, funding and monitoring and evaluation.
- Developing a core management team of selected board members for taking decisions more frequently than meetings of the main board.
- Establishing a system of primary and secondary partners with only primary partners designating board members.
- Setting up parallel participation arrangements for residents and community representatives, such as an inclusive membership citizens' forum which works in cooperation with the regeneration board.

Sometimes the need for reorganisation is so pressing, or so substantial, that the partnership is 'relaunched'. This is taken up in a later section.

Both Manchester City Pride and the Salford Partnership have sought to balance the benefits of an inclusive approach to membership, such as the potential to develop broad consensus among key sectors and players, against the capacity of a small, lean partnership to drive things forward with maximum effectiveness. For City Pride an advisory panel has involved anything up to 75 participants to frame key issues and concerns, but most business is transacted in a much smaller, Executive Committee. In the Salford Partnership there is strong support for maintaining a breadth of involvement, but the need to build a small executive team – a 'group of doers' – is also recognised in order to generate action out of intention. After a reorganisation, the Sheffield First Partnership also identified the need to get 'can do' people on their main board to act as a catalyst to the whole city-wide regeneration programme, excluding those without the 'pulling

power' or the commitment to make the partnership succeed.

The Capital City Partnership (CCP) in Edinburgh also had the problem of too many board members, with numbers gradually climbing to 35 and higher, making meetings unwieldy, discussion less productive and reducing opportunities for any one representative to participate. The CCP brought in independent consultants for a wholesale review of operations, resulting in a streamlined board of directors.

In terms of which kinds of agencies are able to be brought around the partnership table, the general record of partnership is that local authority departments and public and quasi-public agencies such as some TECs/LECs are readily attracted to partnership processes – although the level of commitment varies enormously, particularly with education and social services departments, and it evolves over time.

'Nurturing' for effective partnership operation

Nurturing of partnership, or paying attention to making them work, is a key factor in achieving regeneration objectives. At the outset of partnership, or when partnership working is weak, formal or informal attempts to build mutual understanding among partner agencies can be beneficial. Anyone with a leadership role can also 'nurture' partnerships by informally building bridges with less enthusiastic partners, helping them recognise benefits for their organisation in partnership working.

> Effective partnership often requires the 'nurturing' of relationships among partners and their commitment and ensuring that some flow of benefits to partners runs in parallel to regeneration achievements.

For example, the Glasgow Alliance has attempted a number of approaches to building positive relationships among partners. Presentations by board members about their own organisation's agenda was instigated, based on a recognition that partnership needed to facilitate mutual learning. The process of developing the Alliance's new strategy was also viewed as a useful mechanism for those involved in the

Directors Group – the second tier in the Alliance structure responsible for operational issues. The bones of the strategy were developed in a series of Saturday morning workshops which put specialists together with non-specialists to make linkages across sectors and generate ideas.

In Edinburgh, both the city-wide CCP and the area-based NEAR have taken specific steps to develop relationships between partners and to help foster mutual understanding. CCP was kick-started with a scenario-building exercise, funded by Scottish Homes and intended to perform both team building and visioning functions. However, the impact was limited because of the small number of parties involved, and it was not followed up by further exercises designed to bring new partners on board. In contrast, while there were no attempts at relationship building at the outset in NEAR, new participants are asked to make a presentation about their organisation's responsibilities and culture, and explicit efforts are made to exploit this information for the benefit of the partnership. The full-time manager of NEAR also puts a lot of effort into nurturing the partnership, which has paid dividends.

Typical of many partnerships, the Motherwell North Partnership was formed as a reaction to a competition for central government regeneration resources with little time during an intensive bidding process to consider what might be the most productive way of partnership working. However, since being awarded partnership status, those involved have given priority to developing an appropriate way of working. Thus, a series of 'away days', often using an outside facilitator, have been held on topics such as the role and remit of the board and sub-groups, the role of community representatives, rules and reporting procedures, and staff support for the partnership. These have been complemented with briefings for community representatives and topic seminars focused on the formation of policy in relation to, for example, health and employment. These elements are viewed as a process or development strategy for the partnership

Partnership working can also be encouraged through more formal agreements. For example, the Salford Partnership is now developing a contractual approach which helps to clarify what is expected of partners and ties them explicitly into the regeneration process. Thus, the TEC has signed a 'Statement of Intent', identifying how its

mainstream programmes will impact on the partnership's priority areas. For example, while previously its Modern Apprenticeship scheme was set up in a non-targeted way, it is now committed to generate a number of apprentices in an SRB area. While not a legal contract, this statement constitutes a moral commitment which will help ensure that the TEC delivers. Partnership members are supportive of formalising expectations held of them in this way, as this can help bend mainstream programmes and resources towards regeneration priorities.

High-quality human resources for partnership

Staffing the partnership

A partnership with full-time paid staff, who are able to operate with a degree of independence from any one partner, is likely to deliver more consistently on its strategic programme and make better use of the partnership's human and financial resources. Paid regeneration staff are better able to:

- Encourage the participation of key potential partners in the regeneration partnership by face-to-face meetings as required to build initial bridges.

- Systematically shape the regeneration agenda and provide summarised relevant information at the right time to maximise the efficiency of board and other meetings, and thus of board members' time.

- Represent the partnership in discussion at all levels, with potential funders and other strategic partnerships, thus substantially building the 'networks' of contacts which strengthen partnership.

- Foster communication across line departments in local government, and between agencies, facilitating joined-up action.

Often, in the early days, without dedicated funding, partnerships are run with staff seconded on a part-time basis from other tasks within the lead local authority. Although secondments themselves are of real value, for most partnerships part-time staffing is a second-best option compared with having a modest number of full-time staff, under a chief executive whose time is devoted wholly to the regeneration initiative. There is evidence that just modest salary funding can generate substantial improvements in partnership performance, compared with no funding.

Local partnerships have tended to be more adequately staffed than city-wide and other strategic partnerships. But the situation is changing, and most strategic partnerships now have one or more paid staff.

The importance of staffed partnerships has been formally recognised by the Scottish Executive, which has made Partnership Support Funding grants available to regeneration partnerships at both local and city-wide level. For example, the Motherwell North Partnership did not have a dedicated staff team for the first 18 months of its operation, but was managed by staff from North Lanarkshire Council. A bid to the Scottish Executive for partnership resources was successful and was match-funded by contributions in cash and kind from the public sector partners. A team of 6.5 staff is being hired, including a partnership manager and four development officers. Establishing a dedicated staff team, independent from any one partner, is viewed as essential for the smooth running of this partnership; but considerable discussion has been required over the roles and responsibilities of the new team, over who oversees the work of the team and to whom the team should be responsible.

At the local level in Edinburgh, the NEAR partnership has had a dedicated staff working in a local base since the partnership's inception in 1994. It is clear that benefits have flowed from this facility for the partnership process, including credibility, both locally and externally. The project manager has been able to: facilitate negotiations between partners who had previously not worked together, bring local councillors fully on board, and provide an arena in which partners can float ideas away from the formality of the board room. There is a consensus that providing such opportunities for informal interaction and exchange is important to building effective partnership. The NEAR staff complement has recently been expanded from two to five, meaning that a powerful team is now available to promote the regeneration agenda.

Lead partners in both the Salford Partnership and

Greater Manchester City Pride recognise the value of independent staff, funded preferably through pooling the resources of partners, as a means of building a shared sense of responsibility for the partnership. In both cases, however, the partnerships are struggling to come up with a workable funding model. In the Welsh Valleys Partnership, the need to develop 'regional assessments', leading to a sophisticated Single Programming Document for £1.3 billion of Objective 1 expenditure, has taxed the time resources of the partnership, especially of the two local authority coordinators seconded (only part time) to the task. They have risen to the occasion, but it must be asked whether paid staff with more time available to address the complex challenges of regional development might have brought added value to the task.

An as yet unusual but complementary approach to having a dedicated partnership staff is to make use of specialist managing agents to augment the partnership, either to address technical aspects of the management of funding or to assist in developing a strategic agenda. This is the service offered by Newham's Stratford Development Partnership (SDP), a not-for-profit company with around 40 staff. SDP started as a City Challenge 'delivery agency', working at arm's length from the council, to enable it to challenge the council to bend programmes and services on the basis of its strategic regeneration objectives, a willingness to take risks, and positive links to the local community. Having built a substantial capacity to do so, SDP now works as a regeneration/delivery agency for SRB-funded partnerships in both Newham and surrounding local authorities, transferring learning from one partnership to another and substantially reducing the need for reinventing the wheel with each new input of partnership funding.

Training and the development of personal aptitudes

Partnerships are highly dependent on the quality of their human resources, with a premium on the qualities and skills of partnership members and managers. Even high-quality staff may struggle to meet demands placed on them by the short deadlines of funding regimes and the need to establish commitment to partnership among a variety of stakeholders with organisational cultures as divergent as local authority, police, health authority, business and community.

Important human aspects of partnership working – communication and diplomacy skills, building of trust and mutual understanding, learning how power sharing can increase agency effectiveness and so on – all take time to learn. Confidence building is also important, particularly for board members – while they may be representatives of their stakeholder groups, they need to have the courage and mandate to make and take decisions and accept responsibilities on behalf of their agency in the partnership. Personal skills, which can be developed, ought to be key aspects of selection of regeneration managers, staff and even board members.

An important related task, as yet unaddressed, is to assist local councillors, particularly the great majority now outside of local authority 'cabinets', to rethink their role in partnership and ward representation vis-à-vis the local resident and business community.

Partnership working requires special skills and aptitudes. Members of Sheffield's City Liaison Group (CLG), an early partnership with many problems in overcoming tension between local government and business, agreed as a first step to stop criticising each other in public but to continue to do so in private. This enabled the partnership to tackle their serious disagreements in a more constructive manner while presenting a unified face to the wider world. This demonstrates the need for 'space' for private, difficult conversations enabling resolution. The CLG has been superseded by Sheffield First, but its ability to foster resolution of a long-standing dispute provided a sound foundation for subsequent city-wide partnership. The process highlighted the importance of getting 'the right people' around the table. Leadership qualities are seen as important. As one partner put it: "Good partnership members tend to be blunt, sharp people who get things done, and are determined to drive the agenda".

East London's Thames Gateway Partnership (TGP) came close to being wound up by its local authority funders two years ago due to the failure of the previous management team of the partnership to take a strategic, as opposed to a project-oriented, view of development opportunities and to make positive, 'diplomatic' links with the leaders of its dozen member councils. However a new chief executive hired since, with the appropriate professional and personal skills, has injected vitality and political

commitment into the partnership – suggesting how the skills of a chief executive can make all the difference to partnership. To spread the skills base for partnership working among the many officers and community representatives involved from different local authorities, TGP now organises Best Practice Forums to raise standards, promote skills and to give attendees the chance for 'off the record' discussions away from formal meetings of what works and what doesn't in regeneration practice.

A culture of partnership

Differing organisation cultures, which often clash in the early days of partnership, can be a determinant of the success or otherwise of a partnership. A major task in the early days of partnership is to break down these cultural barriers and mutual suspicions and, sometimes, to circumvent traditional ways of working which are antithetical to partnership.

Local councils in particular have been said to be paternalistic, bureaucratic, power-hungry and controlling. In more than a few cases, local authorities have been perceived as wanting to use partnership mainly to secure much needed central funding and deliver their own preconceived programmes, with no real willingness to negotiate or compromise so that the needs and interests of other partners are taken into account. The emergence of successful partnership working is very often conditional on a change of attitudes and practices within the local authority, which can trigger change in other partner organisations.

Partnerships need to be learning organisations: not only about success and failure in regeneration strategy, by monitoring, but equally about the underlying attitudes and values, reflected in working practices that partners bring to the table. These are the indicators of organisational culture, which can be gradually and constructively shifted to embrace and reward partnership working. There are some formal, but many informal, ways to do this.

Of great significance to partnership is the recent process of local government modernisation and implementation of the Best Value agenda. This is fostering major, positive shifts in the organisational culture of many local authorities. It is taken up in Chapter 4.

For example, although it has been successful in partnerships to promote flagship regeneration projects, Birmingham struggled in the past to develop a comprehensive economic regeneration policy for the city. There was a strong feeling of non-council partners that the council was being reluctant to 'give any power away' on such matters. A changed leadership of the council and the advent of a new economic development partnership marked a changing organisational culture. The establishment of the Regeneration Policy Review Panel also indicates this change, with the local authority now inviting citizens and professionals to comment critically on its approach to partnership and regeneration. The Panel is also charged with determining key relationships among partner agencies, such as TEC and Chamber, and also with clarifying relationships among council, City Pride partnership, Government Offices for the Regions and the RDA.

The case of Rhondda Cynon Taff also shows how organisational culture can shift rapidly. Previous attempts to foster partnership were hindered by an innate suspicion of change and a preponderance of 'old style' local councillors who felt that their status depended less on partnership than on maintaining what political control was available to them. A wholesale change in party control in the 1999 local government elections, coupled with a dynamic programme of a new chief executive, has brought new opportunities for establishing development partnerships. In a new five-year corporate plan, 'Breathing New Life', the leader and chief executive put forward proposals for developing shared vision around economic development, environmental improvement, social development, health and community pride. Strategy is linked to 'action points' and five-year targets. To enhance its partnership capabilities by joined-up government, an internal strategic coordination group has been established to provide a coherent local government approach to a new multi-agency Strategic Renewal Partnership. The need for such change in the Welsh Valleys is pressing. The Arts Factory, discussed above, considering prospects for partnership under Objective 1, states:

> "Previous programmes said the right thing about the need for effective partnerships ... but it rarely happened in practice. Considerable resources will need to be devoted to building the capacity of these partnerships."

Relaunching partnership

Partnerships can and do lose direction, or fall apart, from public squabbling between partners who fail to develop a common agenda, or fail for many other reasons. Some are wound up, but this is not a viable option for visible, city-wide partnerships. Failure of partnership is not a crime, but it is important that lessons of experience be learned and dealt with in an honest manner and that new, effective ways of working are set in place before a partnership is relaunched. A relaunch can be a good way to focus hearts and minds on the necessary steps. This reinforces the need for partnerships to see themselves as 'learning organisations'.

An unexpected finding of the research was the importance of relaunching partnerships that have failed in the past or which, more commonly, have lost their sense of direction and remit, but are still required. In so doing, it is important to take measures to enhance credibility and ensure that the lessons of experience have been learned and acted upon. Three major city-wide partnerships were recently formally relaunched: Sheffield First, Birmingham City Pride and the Glasgow Alliance. The second prospectus of Manchester City Pride could be said to represent an informal relaunch.

In the case of Sheffield First, it was necessary to restore local confidence that the city-wide partnership was promoting a coherent approach. In relaunching, partners were keen to raise its profile by changing the name and by branding it more simply. The importance of being associated with practical success was also highlighted. particularly to promote inward investment. "It's about promoting the city and achieving something real" (partner). There is a perceived need to be honest about past failures and to be 'up front' about how partnership is changing. The organisation of a community conference was important to raising confidence – "We spent a fortune, it was a Rolls Royce event", in the words of one local activist.

Birmingham City Pride also required a relaunch. The long-standing partnership had been established for five years. After initial enthusiasm, it lost direction and a defined role, particularly since City Pride status carried no dedicated funding. As a result, the partnership went through a period of restructuring and consolidation. The relaunched City Pride is now a voluntary arrangement between all city-wide agencies and organisations that have strategic roles covering the whole of the city, including, the council, the TEC, the Chamber, Birmingham City 2000 – the city-centre business organisation, the Voluntary Services Council, the health authority, Birmingham Social Housing Partnership, the university sector, West Midlands Police and the Birmingham Marketing Partnership. The key to the relaunch is that a new membership structure ensures that the partnership is not seen to be in control of any one body. The independence of the partnership is critical to its ability to act as the custodian of the 'city's vision'.

3

Joined-up partnerships: a chain as strong as its weakest link

In the 10 years since partnership has become a mainstay of regeneration efforts, there has been progress in linking partners across sectors: local authority, TEC/LEC, health authority, police, voluntary and community organisations and so on. This is horizontal integration, which defines the current approach to multi-agency partnership (see Carley and Christie, 1992, for a discussion of the terms horizontal and vertical integration). This type of integration could also be about linking partnerships, for example between neighbourhoods. Horizontal integration is necessary, but usually not sufficient, to achieve long-lasting regeneration within the context of effective use of limited resources.

Vertical integration is also necessary to enhance partnership regeneration at all levels. This means positive, supportive linkage between neighbourhood, city, sub-regional and regional partnerships – all supported by national urban policy.

This requirement is reflected in the cluster approach to this study. Sometimes the term 'subsidiarity' is used to describe this vertical chain of partnership, governance and policy – which is only as strong as its weakest link. This vertical integration is essential to link bottom-up and top-down initiatives in a coherent whole, so that all are pulling in the same direction rather than at cross-purposes. Subsidiarity also implies that decisions are pushed down the chain and taken at the appropriate spatial level. For example, policies for *neighbourhood* regeneration ought to be framed in a neighbourhood-level partnership. But if they are to be effective they will need to be supported at the *area* level, where services and service budgets are often organised; and at the *city* level, so that regeneration in one neighbourhood isn't just pushing problems

elsewhere and so there is a positive reinforcement between development plans in one part of the city and another.

Local partnerships also need to be supported by strategic partnerships at a *sub-regional* and/or *regional level*, so that, for example, new factory location, transport infrastructure investments, house building on greenfield sites, new retailing sites and any developments in adjacent local authorities, even housing association developments, are coordinated to good purpose. Without this spatial coordination of partnership and governance, there is too much chance of wasting scarce resources, including much needed inward investments, desperately needed to counteract decades of industrial decline. These linkages are illustrated in Figure 4.

It is not only the existence of partnership at various levels but their effectiveness in terms of their regeneration strategy and ways of working that is important. This chapter considers:

- joined-up local partnerships within, and between, local authorities;
- strategic partnerships at the city-wide level;
- linkage between city-wide and sub-regional partnerships.

Chapters 3 and 5 can be read together: Chapter 5 looks at how regional governance is supporting partnership efforts.

Local partnerships

There is growing interest in neighbourhoods as a focus of local regeneration efforts, not least because of the Prime Minister's interest in the developing national strategy for neighbourhood renewal, *Bringing Britain together* (SEU, 1998). But, as noted above, neighbourhood partnerships may depend in part on their integration into area and city-wide efforts. (An 'area' in this report is a logical grouping of neighbourhoods or wards. Although local residents may prefer to participate at neighbourhood level, services are often best organised at area level, and the two perspectives must be accommodated.) Some people involved in neighbourhood efforts can also become involved at the area level, thus both broadening their understanding of the more strategic dimensions of neighbourhood renewal and providing a personal linkage between levels of effort. Communication between locally based partnerships can foster learning-by-doing and be useful for confidence building among community groups engaged in similar regeneration challenges. At the local level, multi-authority partnerships may also become more common.

A good example of this linkage is provided by long-standing regeneration efforts in North Edinburgh. There is a high degree of integration between two related local partnerships in the Edinburgh case study: the Pilton Partnership, representing the community in six neighbourhoods, and mainly concerned with community development and anti-poverty measures, and North Edinburgh Area Renewal – the NEAR Project – a social inclusion partnership. NEAR has a more strategic and comprehensive role in North Edinburgh's regeneration; it links the community to institutional stakeholders through its representation in the city-wide Capital City Partnership, and to the wider area through, for example, its involvement in the Granton Partnership, which intends to redevelop a large piece of foreshore adjacent to Pilton as a new, sustainable urban community of 5,000 residents. This linkage of levels through partnership structures enables residents of Pilton to have some influence on policies and developments that, although not in Pilton, will have a substantial affect on Pilton, for better or worse (Carley, 1997).

The good working relationship that exists between the Pilton Partnership and NEAR has been achieved partly through informal processes; for example, there is considerable crossover of the individuals involved, which extends to councillors, officers and community representatives. Importantly, a mechanism has been developed which allows NEAR's strategic priorities to be delivered partly through a Pilton Urban Aid Panel, the membership of which is local community representatives, supported by officers. This allows urban aid – a key element of the special regeneration resources available to NEAR – to be disbursed according to a community-based process, but with clear reference to the need to mesh with NEAR's strategic objectives. There is also an opportunity for community reps to input into determining NEAR's strategic objectives, through direct involvement on the NEAR board and sub-groups.

Partnerships between local authorities are not new, but the Cheetham and Broughton Partnership (CBP) is a rare example of two authorities, Manchester City and Salford, working together at the neighbourhood level across boundaries – the first joint partnership under SRB. One lesson from the partnership is that partners need to demonstrate abilities at joint working quickly to overcome what may be long-ingrained mutual suspicion. CBP is only now, after two years, beginning to develop trust and mutual confidence at its steering group level. Senior officer relations are good, although even here "we are not yet prepared to be open enough with each other", and an ethic of joint working still has to percolate through to front-line officers. The SRB team is seen as belonging to Manchester – although it is responsible for coordinating appraisals and reports on activities across the area – and Salford has its own staff. Establishing a team for the partnership that is accepted to both principal partners and to outside bodies should be a priority. In this case, a legal structure may be required to create genuine joint ownership.

Area initiatives and locality budgeting

There is growing recognition of the need to harness mainstream budgets and services to social inclusion requirements, given that more than 90% of public expenditure in regeneration areas is through mainstream budgets in what have been called 'silos' or vertical structures of government. Such services are traditionally planned and implemented by a single central government department and its relevant local agency or local government department. These include: education, health, enterprise and skills development, housing and income support and other areas. For deprived areas, mainstream programmes need to achieve better integration with each other and within the context of regeneration programme funding, such as for Scotland's Social Inclusion Partnerships.

Figure 4: Vertical integration – a chain of partnership only as strong as its weakest link

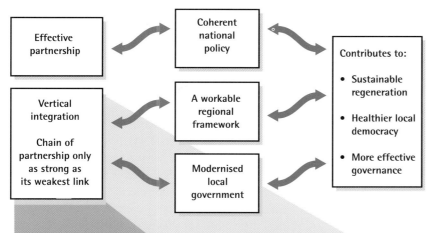

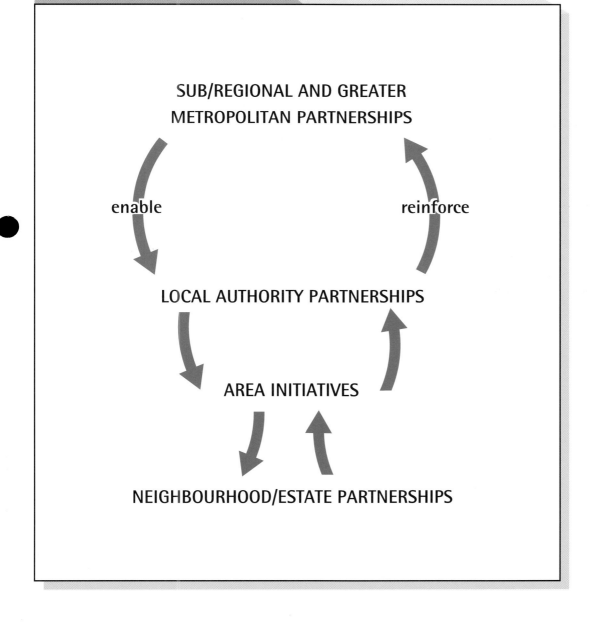

The Scottish Executive's recent statement, *Social justice ... a Scotland where everyone matters* (1999), identifies the need to integrate across budget streams, both nationally and locally. For the latter, a budgetary system that is responsive to community preferences and local requirements is needed. The statement notes that, on current arrangements, "partnership action may be frustrated by local budgetary processes", including mismatch between available budgets and needed pattern of spend and by lack of relevant spending powers at the local level.

The notion of 'bending' mainstream budgets to achieve additional benefits in regeneration areas has long been identified as important, but recently more practical attempts have begun to be made to achieve such integration. If it is to be achieved, one of the first tasks of any partnership is to make progress towards the concept of *coordinated locality budgeting*. This involves knowing what the level of public expenditure is in any service sector in a designated regeneration area, as a first important step to adjusting diverse budgets which impact on individuals, households and the community. The purpose is to achieve additional regeneration benefits and an improved quality of life from a process of coordinating resource commitments, linking them to regeneration objectives and systematically monitoring the outcomes of expenditure patterns. Locality budgeting can be a powerful tool not only to assist local partnerships, but to ensure more efficient monitoring of expenditure as a whole by providing bottom-up assessment of top-down expenditure. However, it needs to extend beyond the local authority budgets to encompass all public expenditure in an area.

Financial expenditure: feedback from partnership to policy

Top-down policy frameworks can only benefit from an increased flow of information (or intelligence) from the front lines of partnership and service delivery, so that policy can be refined and tailored to better meet objectives intended to reduce social exclusion. This is another component of the chain of sustainable regeneration.

In Scotland, partnership at the *area* level to work toward locality budgeting, and to support neighbourhood initiatives, is being developed in Edinburgh as part of the Scottish Executive's social inclusion initiatives (Scottish Executive, 1999). A West Edinburgh Pilot project, in an area including the 26 neighbourhoods of the flagship Wester Hailes Partnership but also other residential and commercial areas, is examining financial inputs for key activities in the area, including local economic development, community care and lifelong learning. The revenue expenditure in the area amounts to £44 million per year, with substantial scope for 'bending' funding for regeneration and quality-of-life objectives. The first step is to identify spending by all the various public sector organisations in the area, to help communities, local agencies and regeneration partnerships get maximum benefit from public expenditure patterns.

In East London, Britain's first Social Enterprise Zone (SEZ) in Newham's Forest Gate – Plaistow Sustainable Communities (SRB) Partnership – intends to find innovative new ways to use mainstream budgets to tackle multiple deprivation, not only working in a broad-based local partnership, but lobbying directly to central government as required, thus drawing central departments more closely into practical, local partnership action (Robinson et al, 1998; Community Links, 1999). The SEZ hopes to change rules and regulations to benefit the local community and economy and to promote the reinvestment of efficiency savings directly back in the community. Working in an area with great ethnic diversity and much low-quality private rented accommodation, its first proposals are for reinvestment of VAT on new building in a community development fund.

City-wide partnerships

Following the development of multi-agency partnerships for urban regeneration in the 1980s, an important innovation during the 1990s has been the evolution of a city-wide perspective on regeneration. This approach usually encompasses both the organisational framework, in terms of a city-wide partnership of key stakeholders, and the spatial focus of the regeneration strategy at the city level. The city-wide approach then provides the context for area-based, estate and neighbourhood regeneration (Community Links, 1999; Carley and Kirk, 1999).

In Scotland, Programme for Partnership encouraged participating cities to enter into partnership and develop city-wide strategies to provide a strategic framework for area regeneration in Priority Partnership Areas, now evolved into SIPs. Following this, the First Minister announced the availability of earmarked funds for providing staff for city-wide and other partnerships under Partnership Support Funding Grants.

For England and Wales, city-wide approaches have been encouraged by the City Pride Initiative and by the Single Regeneration Budget (SRB). City Pride was initiated in late 1993 in Manchester, Birmingham and London at the invitation of the Secretary of State for the Environment, for partner agencies in those cities to come together to take a 10-year perspective on regeneration. The City Pride approach was to have been extended to an additional seven designated cities. However, it has now been superseded by New Commitment to Regeneration – Pathfinder Initiatives coordinated by the Local Government Association (LGA) with the DETR.

At this spatial level, the case studies demonstrate a general clarity about the need to have one or at best two city-wide partnerships and no more, recognising that too many partnerships can be almost as bad as too few. At the city-wide level, the tendency is to start with a partnership focused on city-wide regeneration and then to complement this with a general urban development partnership concerned with the broadest issues of strategic development. In the concluding chapter of this report we will suggest that regeneration should always be carried within a broader urban development framework, and in this sense a blurring of the edges of strategic partnerships is entirely appropriate.

At the city-wide level, some cities see it in their interest to bring together a general urban development partnership concerned with the broadest issues of strategic development, to complement the city-wide regeneration partnership.

In cities like Glasgow, Manchester, Birmingham and the London Borough of Newham, all with a high degree of deprivation and a majority of residents living in designated regeneration areas, tasks of urban development and regeneration overlap to a great extent, and separate city-wide partnerships for regeneration and urban

development have not been seen to be required. The tasks become interchangeable: Glasgow's Regeneration Alliance has dropped the 'regeneration' label; Newham's Chief Executive's Forum is about all aspects of quality of life in London's most deprived borough – but where many residents, it must be noted, will not be deprived and where general prosperity and a healthy mix of working and middle-class residents is the longer-term vision. In Manchester, City Pride has evolved from its original regeneration focus to encompass the overall development of the city's economic and social life, vital in turn to regeneration at city, area and neighbourhood levels.

Similarly, generally prosperous Edinburgh started with the Capital City Partnership for regeneration, first unfunded and staffed from the local authority. Later a modest amount of funding was made available to hire a chief executive. It also became apparent that there were visions and aspirations for the city that had little to do with funded regeneration programmes but were more generally focused on overall prosperity, quality-of-life and sustainable development issues. A high level Edinburgh Partnership of mainly chief executives was established to address these broad, strategic issues, but also to provide a context for city-wide and local regeneration efforts, which depend very much on a city's general prosperity to support regeneration aspirations.

Sub–regional partnerships in a regional context

The case studies reveal a complex situation at this spatial level. This ranges from one extreme in East London, where the former chief executive of Newham complains of "innumerable uncoordinated structures at the sub-regional level", to Sheffield, with appropriate partnerships at regional and sub-regional levels. At the other extreme, in the Welsh Valleys, a single working, regional partnership, remaining to be further formalised and developed in response to Objective 1 designation, cannot, at least in the short term, make up for the imposition of relatively small, single-tier local government at the last reorganisation, resulting in a lack of more formal regional planning and economic development framework to coordinate regeneration across the Valleys.

A difficult situation at this other extreme occurs in the urban west of central Scotland, encompassing Greater Glasgow and neighbouring local authorities, such as Renfrewshire and North Lanarkshire, whose need for regeneration is of an equal magnitude to Glasgow's. Here, as in Wales, local government reorganisation left a regional planning vacuum. There are no sub-regional partnerships as yet developed to provide a context for the regeneration of Glasgow. Major industrial developments in North Lanarkshire are inaccessible by public transport from Glasgow peripheral estates such as Easterhouse – only a few miles away by motorway. Not only is there no sub-regional partnership, but Glasgow itself finds that local government reorganisation under the Conservatives hived off some of its prosperous suburbs.

> In Scotland and Wales, local government reorganisation which imposed single-tier local government, has left a regional planning vacuum which tends to weaken regeneration efforts that ought to be taking place in a logical travel-to-work, or greater metropolitan, area and reduces the effectiveness of efforts at the local authority level. Inter-authority partnerships have yet to fill this vacuum.

For England, and despite the advantages being conferred by the regional structures, there is strong feeling among members of strategic partnerships that central government ought to do more to promote and support sub-regional partnership structures in urban areas that contain multiple local authorities. City Pride was felt to be a good start in this regard, bringing together, for example, four local authorities in Manchester which were unlikely to have come together otherwise. The abandoned second round of City Pride designations, which encouraged further inter-local authority cooperation, no doubt would have supported more such sub-regional partnerships, such as the Greater Nottingham Partnership of six local authorities.

Hurdles and added value in inter-authority partnerships

Effective inter-authority partnerships at this sub-regional level face a number of hurdles:

- Traditional rivalry between local authorities, often either equally deprived, and thus competing for the same regeneration funding and/or the same inward investment, or rich and poor areas, at odds over rates and local authority expenditure.
- A tendency for the largest local authority to dominate the partnership.
- The fact that only a modest percentage of the large numbers of local councillors have the skills or inclination to engage in the kind of strategic thinking that underpins sub-regional regeneration.
- Project-oriented thinking.

And yet, this sub-regional level of partnership is vital, because:

- Economic planning and regeneration and enhancement of employment opportunities (both people to jobs and jobs to people) are most efficiently carried out at the level of the 'travel-to-work' region.
- There is a need to counteract the fall of urban populations and shift of employment and economic function from city to suburb as jobs, shops and homes continue a trend of decentralisation to greenfield and rural locations.
- It is vital to achieve multiplier benefits between urban regeneration and the need for sustainable development, for example to concentrate population so that public transport is a feasible financial and social alternative to car use. This is important given that residents of regeneration areas invariably have low levels of car ownership.

Conversely, there is good evidence that sub-regional partnership provides added value in the integration of the above factors. For example, the Thames Gateway Partnership "supports strategic objectives between its 12 member local authorities, and local regeneration objectives within local authorities". Its sub-regional focus is specifically on economic development, land use planning and investment in transport, education and other infrastructure to support that economic development. Many of these infrastructure projects, such as the new University of East London campus at London City Airport in Docklands, have real potential to foster regeneration. Within the spatial context of Thames Gateway, the Regeneration Best Value Chain devised by the London Borough of Newham specifically examines actions and programmes at the national, sub-regional and borough levels for what is called their 'flow-through impact' on local partnerships.

The North East has a long-standing commitment to sub-regional partnership working. The key sub-regional partnership for the Tees Valley has been the Tees Valley Joint Strategy Unit (TVJSU). This represents a joint effort of five local authorities on strategic planning, transport and regional economic development. To work towards an economically competitive future for the region, a new partnership is being established: this is the Tees Valley Partnership, which will use the capacity of TVJSU as its secretariat and will link directly with Tees Valley Tomorrow, the lead private sector partnership.

● *Boundaries for sub-regional partnerships*

Appropriate boundaries are important to sub-regional partnerships to ensure that an effective geographic area is defined for economic and social development. But appropriate boundaries may not always be obvious at first, although a travel-to-work area, where easily defined, is a good starting point for a tentative sub-regional partnership. Political commitment is as important as spatial logic, however, and it is often logical for boundaries to evolve as local authorities find it in their interests to join with neighbouring local authorities to pursue common interests, especially economic regeneration. With the advent of RDAs (and the potential demise of TECs), there is real concern that successful sub-regional partnerships, with their valuable human and information networks, could be undermined by obscuring them under regional interests and/or by direct financial links between grant-dispensing RDAs and large, cash-strapped local authorities.

It is not only the boundaries of regeneration partnerships, but their 'fit' with other administrative boundaries, that is important to effective regeneration. For example, given the fragmented nature of governance across Greater Manchester, it is perhaps surprising that the City Pride area of operation has been coterminous with those of the Manchester TEC and the Manchester Chamber of Commerce, with undoubted benefits for developing partnership at the sub-regional level. Within this context, however, recent initiatives such as the plans to disband TECs, and the establishment of new 'zones' on health and education, are in danger of undermining the potential to develop a coherent

sub-regional focus unless the issue of boundaries is dealt with at a regional level.

In East London, the Thames Gateway Partnership now has ministerial backing, and that of local council leaders, to work to remedy London's West–East imbalance in prosperity and to address the fact that East London may well have too many uncoordinated sub-regional regeneration initiatives with varying boundaries. "Thames Gateway is not about projects but about the big picture for the sub-region", with officer-led task groups on skills, transport, environment and industry and financial services.

Section III: The foundations of partnerships

4

The modernisation of local government

The research found that local councils which are the lead agency in major regeneration partnerships increasingly recognise the potential for a powerful linkage between their modernisation agenda and better partnership working. In the past, many non-local authority partners cited lack of joined-up policy and practice within local authorities and inter-departmental rivalry, or at least lack of communication between departments, as significant barriers to effective partnership. Now partners from business to community and voluntary organisations find that councils which are embracing the changes in the organisational culture and working practices that are at the heart of this agenda are certainly easier to work with – and, it is hoped, will make better, more committed, partners.

Vision and modernisation

The development of new structures of urban governance is, in part, driven by a need for cities like Birmingham, Sheffield and Middlesbrough to respond to global economic competition and rapid social and economic change. To offer the highest quality of life to citizens and inward investors, key city stakeholders have recognised the need for a city-wide vision, that is, a long-term view of where the city is going. The vision is based on partnership and will be developed, shared and delivered by business, public agencies and local communities alike. To lead on the city vision in Birmingham for example, firm political support has been given to City Pride as the lead agency. Also, there is a real sense that Best Value is a potent driver for change. It is no longer a question of who delivers local services, but rather how best to deliver them. This is reflected in the support from the council to the review of the

Many aspects of the *modernisation of local government* agenda are seen to be benefiting regeneration partnerships:

- City visioning processes driven by the council leader builds consensus of partners around long-term development.

- An inter-departmental, 'corporate approach' to policy, planning and budgeting.

- Cabinet-style decision making.

- Streamlining of committee structures, often on thematic lines.

- A stronger role for a coordinating chief executive's department.

- Better local democracy, including area forums and neighbourhood service centres.

- The application of Best Value principles to service delivery and to regeneration programmes themselves.

Modernisation, with its explicit link to both better value in service delivery and improvements in local democracy, is also serving the interests of local neighbourhood and residents' groups, fostering partnership between town hall and neighbourhood. Many residents very sensibly want to see commitments to improved quality of existing service delivery before allocating time to discussion of strategic regeneration issues.

Birmingham Economic Development Partnership in adopting new approaches to joint service provision (see Figure 5).

Innovation in local government

Where regeneration partnerships are being steadily improved, and regeneration initiatives are complemented by broader concern for quality-of-life issues that affect residents of regeneration areas just as much (if not more so) as residents of prosperous neighbourhoods, there is frequently a high degree of initiative in modernisation. For example, the London Borough of Newham sees itself as being "at the leading edge of British local government", having established a Performance and Efficiency Panel as early as 1996. There is evidence that Newham is pushing at the boundaries of innovation in many areas (London Borough of Newham, 1999). Many respondents concerned with regeneration at the local authority level cite the council's modernisation programme, and the commitment of both leader and chief executive to it, as a key to improving the quality and effectiveness of partnership.

One Newham initiative is applying Best Value principles to a review of the council's entire regeneration and partnerships programme. The Best Value team reviews council expenditure on partnerships and regeneration, in part by reference to effective programmes in other local authorities, and reallocates resources for

Figure 5: Modernised local government

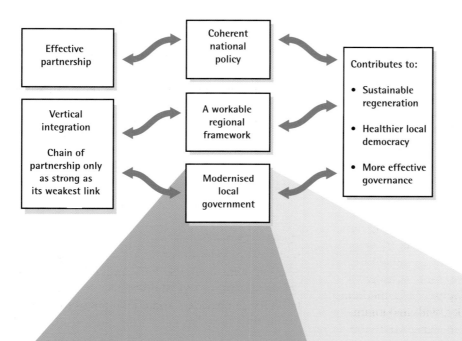

Key points

- Visionary council leadership

- Clear corporate approach

- Regeneration within a strong Chief Executive's Department

- Embrace of a modernisation agenda including new positive role for local councillors outside the 'cabinet'

- Empowerment of local neighbourhoods on a systematic basis with a clear role in community planning and service quality assessment maximum effectiveness, for example firmly withdrawing from a failing inter-authority inward investment partnership (the Lee Valley Partnership), and using the freed resources to increase staffing working on European funding bids. With regard to monitoring of regeneration, the 'output' monitoring required by SRB is to be complemented with 'outcome/impact' monitoring, focused on: a strengthened economy, improved quality of life across the borough and better access to jobs, education and training. These tie together in a Regeneration Impact Model of benchmarking, baseline performance indicators and improvement targets.

● In Rhondda Cynon Taff District Council political change is leading to a changing organisational culture. A change of executive leadership has coincided with a change in ruling party to create real opportunities for modernisation. Recognising that developing a unified strategic approach across the local authority would be a major contribution to partnership, the council is developing a corporate planning approach, backed up by a cabinet style of decision making and a revised committee structure. The local authority sees itself as engaged in "a total restructuring of the authority to give added value to statutory services through Best Value".

● Under the Best Value approach in Birmingham, the city council has instigated a series of Policy Review Panels which are to learn from past experience and 'open up' council policy making to public discussion. For part of their work, the review panels will act like select committees, taking evidence from agencies and individual experts. The first of three panels, the Futures Panel, will look at the development of a medium to long-term vision for the city, with maximum public involvement; the panel is chaired by the leader of the council. A second panel, the Regeneration Panel, will develop a strategic approach to regeneration; departments, agencies and local communities will be encouraged to present evidence and views. The final panel, An Ageing Population, will identify and review both the needs of older people and the broader impact of an ageing population on the city.

Community participation in modernisation and governance

Many representatives of community organisations are reasonably less interested in participating in what they see as one regeneration initiative after another, and rather more interested in direct participation in local government and the evaluation of service delivery, which could include regeneration services.

The role of communities or neighbourhoods in local governance is a keenly felt issue which will need to be addressed both within the modernisation agenda and within the national strategy for neighbourhood renewal. There is a growing range of innovation. For example, Middlebrough proposes four Local Partnership Forums (LPFs) to group existing community councils, which have slightly reorganised to coordinate with ward boundaries. The purpose of the LPFs is to provide a means for wider consultation on key strategic issues and a more focused use of resources for community development. The LPFs, with council funding, would appoint their own chair, secretary, treasurer and officers and develop their own terms of reference. The council in turn will appoint a lead officer to be 'key interface' between residents and the council's policy process. Support will be provided through a funded worker for each LPF. LPF chairs and vice chairs will comprise a town-wide Partnership Forum and will work with leader and commissioners on regeneration and Best Value. The Forum will link to an Assembly, a public body for widespread debate on key issues. Another connection will be between LPFs and the city-wide partnership, Middlesbrough Direct, to link service providers and communities to review programmes objectives and targets. Each LPF will be invited to produce its community plan to inform the overall Middlesbrough Community Plan, which in turn will provide an agenda for Middlesbrough Direct.

Similar innovation combining participation in regeneration and local goverance are found in other areas. In Newham six Community Forums are being established, each to be linked to an area Community Service Centre providing a one-stop shop for interaction between council and community. In Sheffield the council has a pilot initiative – 12 panels representing 'natural neighbourhoods' as opposed to wards. The panels are developing action plans and promoting active community engagement which could evolve into more formal linkage. Council service provision is said to be "naturally restructuring around these areas" but requires a system of devolved budgeting to progress further.

In Birmingham, efforts to strengthen bottom-up approaches to partnership are in parallel to the development of the city-wide strategy. Local Involvement Local Action (LILA) is an initiative developed by the city council to actively involve local people in council decision making. LILA is intended to ensure that the council is more responsive to the needs, concerns and priorities of local people. The council has made £50,000 available to each of the 39 wards in the city. Ward sub-committees and advisory boards identify local solutions to local problems, and ward development plans prioritise local needs and identify appropriate responses, given the resources available. The intention is for an improved framework of service delivery going beyond council services to involve other service providers. LILA also creates an opportunity for local people to participate in, and provide feedback to, the city-wide vision, objectives and indicators. While LILA has many strengths, the success of the initiative is dependent on the ability of organisations within the wards to take forward the initiative.

Democratic deficit and local governance

Extrapolating from existing best practice in the case studies, the research team suggests that the best approaches to community participation in future will involve an integration between the short-term participation exercises of regeneration and improvements in local democratic processes at the neighbourhood and area levels. These can provide substantial support to local partnership action, and address issues of *democratic deficit* which plagues governments in Britain. Democratic deficit locally can be about the quality of local representation and dissatisfaction with the quality of local services, from road sweeping to council house maintenance, but it can also be about the inability to influence that service delivery in a positive fashion. One indicator of democratic deficit is poor turnouts at local elections – often less than 20%. It is important that all efforts at community participation move beyond the lip service that has characterised too

many efforts in past, and that genuine practical participation, in regeneration and otherwise, addresses not only pressing issues but the process of governance itself.

One aspect to consider more clearly is the relationship of the community to its elected representatives. To benefit both partnerships and community, a key task, yet unaddressed, is to redefine the tasks of local councillors, particularly the majority who are now outside the new, inner cabinet structure, to encourage them to play a more positive, sophisticated role as representatives of the community on council, and to integrate partnerships more fully in political decision making.

Another task is to streamline community participation, whether at neighbourhood, area or local authority level, so that there is not an excess of it. Certainly, expectations of the commitment of residents of regeneration areas to participation, often night after night and weekends, is far in excess of what most people will tolerate, which shows when the same few dedicated people show up again and again. A better approach would be to integrate community participation in regeneration partnerships in a broader framework of participation in local governance, the opportunity for which is available across the local authority. Streamlined democratic participation structures across the local authority will carry considerably more political clout than those confined to regeneration areas. The example of Middlesbrough's LPFs indicates how such democratic processes can be initiated.

Good partnerships between local authorities and communities can form around strategic development plans for the neighbourhood and the city rather than solely to secure funding-driven regeneration grants. Formal agreements as to forward action may be necessary to cement partnership arrangements and to demonstrate real commitment of institutional partners to community groups often let down in the past. Revenue as well as capital funding for key community groups could bring real benefits in capacity building. Although deprived areas would obviously have first call on resources, all neighbourhoods should have the opportunity to participate more fully, and more efficiently, in local governance.

5

Regional development

The case for a regional perspective on regeneration

In England, the advent of the Regional Development Agencies (RDAs) and, earlier, the Government Offices for the Regions (GORs) indicates a growing awareness on the part of government of the importance of regional development and partnership to economic and social viability in region, city and neighbourhood. In Wales, the important opportunity of Objective 1 funding over the next seven years has sharpened concern over issues of regional planning and business development and their link to regeneration in the Valleys. In Scotland, an ongoing ESRC-funded study on Cities and Competitiveness is arguing that Glasgow, Edinburgh and communities in between might benefit from a coordinated, rather than a competitive, approach to regional development that places these cities in a common framework (University of Glasgow, 1999).

There is some confusion over terminology, in that Scotland and Wales are frequently referred to as 'regions', just as Northwest England is a region (*The Oxford Dictionary* [1976 edn] defines a region as "a tract of land or a place having more or less definitely marked boundaries or characteristics including flora and fauna"). However it is hard to substantiate, for example, that Scotland is a *single* region, encompassing geographic areas and economies as diverse as the Lowlands, the industrial Central Belt and the Highlands and the Islands – the latter whose residents often express their lack of affinity to a government based in Edinburgh. To be fair, Scotland does have agencies organised at what might be termed a regional level, particularly

Scottish Homes and the Enterprise Network, but these 'regions' are many in number.

However regions are defined, and it ought to be an ongoing matter of public discussion, regional issues are vital to regeneration and partnership. Chapter 3 introduced some key economic and demographic issues arising in a regional context, which can impact on the viability of regeneration partnerships operating at sub-regional, city and local levels. Foremost among these is the shift of economic vitality, jobs, population, shopping, recreational facilities and new housing from urban to suburban and rural areas since 1980.

The legacy of this shift is obvious to regeneration practitioners and urban residents alike: dramatic loss of employment and industrial plant in cities, vast swathes of derelict inner-city of negligible property value, serious loss of inner-city population (a 40% loss, still continuing, in some of the industrial cities studied here), the rundown of inner-city services such as education as enrolments fall but fixed costs remain constant, and what has been called 'area abandonment' of urban neighbourhoods as houses fall vacant and drug dealers and other criminals move in. In the worst hit cities the situation will continue to deteriorate. Many of the cities studied here, although successful in some aspects of regeneration, face such problems on a daily basis.

Regional initiative and coordination is important to regeneration partnership for:

- Promoting economic development which underpins successful regeneration at all levels.

- Coordinating inward investment decisions and public support.

- Providing a coherent land use and development framework for regeneration, for example, to ensure that out-of-town shopping developments do not undermine inner-city regeneration.

- Planning for investment in transport and communications infrastructure which will improve the prospects of regeneration and help Britain reduce CO_2 emissions and meet other sustainability requirements, all of which improve the quality of life and thus urban development potential.

Diverging regional frameworks

Many of these issues require a framework for taking tough regional decisions. Where decisions are avoided, or swept under the carpet, there may be a 'storing up' of problems and a loss of multiplier benefits between investments and initiatives, making partnership work at lower spatial levels more difficult and less productive.

England, Wales and Scotland have diverging experiences of regional coordination, and these are of concern to members of regeneration partnerships. Whereas at one point Wales and Scotland prided themselves on the establishment of the Welsh and Scottish Development Agencies, it is possible that institutional developments under both Tory and Labour governments have set England more firmly on the road to both coherent regional economic development and land use planning, according to sustainability principles, and for the development of civil and/or political organisations that parallel government arrangements and provide opportunity for discussion and debate on regional issues. However, there is uncertainly at the time of this writing over the role of RDAs in regional development and the administration of regeneration funding (see Figure 6).

Diverging events included a process of local government reorganisation which differed substantially in England compared with Scotland and Wales. In the latter cases, single-tier local government was imposed. For example, in Scotland the responsibilities of the large Strathclyde Regional Council were reallocated to nine restructured smaller unitary authorities. A number of these are within a Greater Glasgow conurbation, competing for the same pot of inward investment without any coordinating framework to ensure an optimum flow of benefits at a regional level, or to see that the benefits of inward investment and public investment accrue to disadvantaged households. Although England had seen the earlier demise of the metropolitan counties, the deliberations of the Banham Commission left two thirds of England with two tiers of local government in 1995.

At around the same time, England also saw the establishment of the Government Offices for the Regions (GORs), located in major regional cities such as Manchester and Birmingham. These coordinate at a regional level central government activity in key departments, including the DETR, DfEE and DTI. Staff now provide a 'bridge' between Whitehall, local authorities and regeneration partnership initiatives through a GOR director of regeneration. Staff of these GORs quickly developed a good appreciation of local development and regeneration issues, to the extent that the previous Conservative administration worried that they had "gone native". Recently, for example, the head of the GOR for the North West, described in the press as a "top regional civil servant", agreed to lead East Manchester's new partnership, which takes the form of a regeneration company set up in response to Urban Task Force recommendations (*New Start*, 5 November 1999).

To coordinate land use and transport, the GORs, working with regional assemblies where they exist, prepare Regional Planning Guidance (RPG). This has considerable potential to promote and coordinate regional sustainable development and thus provide a good foundation for sub-regional initiative. The advent of the RDAs may be a further arrow in the quiver of regional coordination, although it remains to be seen if they have the skills and the mandate to link economic development to a framework for tackling social exclusion.

Figure 6: Workable regional framework

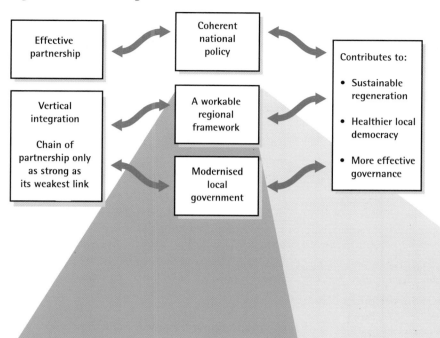

Key points

- Need for overall coherent development framework linking economy, regeneration, social inclusion, transport and land use, and sustainability

- In England, clear, complementary functions for Government Offices, Regional Planning Guidance, Regional Development Agencies, Regional Assemblies, other organisations and (in London) the Mayor's Office

- RDAs should support, rather than threaten, sub-regional partnerships

- More organised institutional framework may be needed in areas of unitary government, especially for Wales and Scotland

In parallel to the establish of GORs, regional organisations emerged, such as, for Greater Manchester, the North West Regional Association of Local Authorities and, for the Sheffield area, the Regional Assembly for Yorkshire and Humberside, consisting of 22 local authority leaders who, among other tasks, oversee the production of RPG and the regional transport strategy. The RPG is intended to "draw together issues such as sustainability, economic growth, regeneration and housing targets". The Assembly has appointed a small staff of strategic planners and administrators. There is also a larger, parallel Chamber which links these leaders to other key regional stakeholders, including representatives of the voluntary sector.

Regional issues in England

Unlike Scotland and Wales, issues in England are less about the need for a regional framework and more about the appropriate role of regional organisations and whether they will mesh to best advantage. For example, there is concern among partnership members in Sheffield, Greater Manchester and East London about the extent to which RPG and the 'Regional Business Plans' of the RDAs will mesh in the coherent manner necessary to support strategic regeneration issues.

For the variety of centrally funded regeneration programmes, a number of senior local authority representatives, including chief executives, feel that GORs should do more to coordinate funding arrangements and monitoring requirements to allow greater impact, and less use of resources for administration, at local level. For some the GORs are a potentially positive force for policy integration, but for others, because they don't include the DTI or the DfEE, they are "another level of uncoordinated bureaucracy at the very time when local authorities are encouraged to put 'joined-up' systems in place".

In Yorkshire and Humberside the GOR is recognised as helpful by regeneration partnership members, although doubts remain as to whether it has improved policy coordination to the extent required. There is concern that the GOR has not been allowed to develop a sophisticated regional development strategy, through RPG or otherwise, and that the RDA's business strategy will be useful but more narrowly focused than programmes for overall regional development and social inclusion ought to be. The Chamber for Yorkshire and Humberside is intended to oversee the work of the RDA and consists of 22 local authority leaders and 13 regional stakeholders. This should certainly provide a necessary measure of democratic accountability to the work of the RDA, but it does not guarantee coordination between RDA and GOR, or between business development, sustainable land use and transport planning and regeneration.

Similar institutional concerns are expressed by London partnership members. With the arrival of both the London Development Agency (LDA) and a Mayor's Office, strategic governance for East London, and thus the conditions under which sub-regional and local authority partnerships operate, is changing fast. Local partnerships feel that care should be exercised to ensure complementary functions – among the Government Office for London (GOL), LDP, Mayor's Office and the East London office of English Partnerships – in such a way as to support existing sub-regional and local partnerships. Currently, both sub-regional and local authority regeneration partnerships are critical of the failure of English Partnerships to define a role for itself beyond packaging of brownfield land for development without, they argue, due consideration of the potential economic and social ramifications.

The Mayor's Office is likely to define an East London sub-region that formally links City of London with the eastern boroughs – a potentially exciting strategic development, but one that suggests the need for extending an existing

partnership structure, such as Thames Gateway, to that spatial level. At this sub-regional level, there are already a number of partnerships, and with the advent of RDAs, there may be a risk of 'partnership proliferation'.

As the role of the GOL is unclear vis-à-vis other regional bodies and local partnerships, so it is unclear as to whether Regional Planning Guidance (RPG) will continue to provide an overall coherence to (sustainable) development in East London, and thus to provide a development framework within which local partnerships develop regeneration strategies. Currently the sub-regional planning guidance that the area benefits from is said to be a powerful, coherent factor, in land use and transport decisions which support regeneration.

Regional issues for Wales and Scotland

Regional development efforts in Wales and Scotland, at the level of the Valleys or Scotland's Central Belt, ought to underpin the work of regeneration partnerships at city and local levels. But these regions lack the advantages conferred by the establishment in England of GORs, RDAs and the mediation processes that underpin RPG. It may be a mistake to assume that, because they are smaller countries in population terms, the Scottish Executive or Offices of the National Assembly for Wales can or will fulfil this regional development and coordination role, or that it can be filled by the business support-focused Welsh Development Agency or Scottish Enterprise. Partnership at the regional level may be necessary.

In Wales and Scotland, one effect of both single-tier local government reorganisation and a lack of an institutional framework similar to GORs and RDAs is that a regional leadership mantle falls directly on the offices of the National Assembly for Wales and the Scottish Executive. To date respondents suggest they have not risen to this task. What is suggested is that they:

- be politically confident of their necessary strategic roles, or delegate responsibility to a strategic planning organisation which can fulfil that role;
- develop and share good information systems on regional development;

- assign sufficient human resources to regional planning and/or allow their officials a break from a 'fire-fighting' style of administration to engage in strategic thinking;
- be prepared to mediate over regional decisions, such as out-of-town shopping centre or greenfield business park location, before decisions need to be taken to the stage of a planning inquiry.

The Welsh Local Government Association goes further, suggesting that, in the face of a "plethora of regional groupings" Wales "may have to reinvent something like county councils by the back door – but without democratic accountability". For Objective 1 planning the Valleys Partnership is local authority-led and driven, its partners engaged in a regional assessment. But, in the absence of a more formal regional structure among the nine constituent local authorities, this partnership has not been able to develop an overall, consensual, politically acceptable economic development strategy or the equivalent of RPG.

Of course, the more formalised English regional structures are far from perfect, and, it could be argued, informal arrangements and networks in Wales and Scotland will do the job. Certainly the Welsh and the Scots will devise their own regional arrangements. But these will need to satisfy requirements for strategic analysis, forward planning and mediation between local authorities over difficult development decisions, leavened with a measure of democratic accountability, however devised. They also ought to provide an appropriate framework for coordinating regeneration strategy, labour market analysis, inward investment and transport and land use planning at the level of travel-to-work areas. Formal arrangements in this regard tend to be more transparent and thus more open to productive discussion and debate over their effectiveness.

6

Supporting partnership with a coherent national policy framework

Instigating partnership

Central government policy in England, Scotland and Wales plays an important catalytic role in encouraging the establishment of partnerships. This is either through direct funding requirements, such as SRB or SIP funding for area regeneration partnerships, or by making partnership a precondition of funding from other programmes, as with City Pride and now New Commitment to Regeneration.

Some senior local authority politicians suggest that central government's "virtually compulsory requirements for partnership were absolutely necessary to foster political change" in the local authority. Other central programmes and legislation, such as funding to establish Health Action Zones or the Community Safety Plans under the 1998 Crime and Disorder Act also instigate valuable partnership efforts which have, over time, genuinely encouraged a culture of joint working among key stakeholders.

Central government plays an important role in encouraging partnership through regeneration funding programmes. But government could do more to foster good practice with the leverage this funding allows: to encourage and reward inter-local authority joint working at sub-regional levels, such as with City Pride, and at neighbourhood levels over local boundaries, such as in the Cheetham and Broughton Partnership; to encourage innovation in local government modernisation which promotes regeneration and community participation; and to encourage administrative practices, such as area-based budgeting, that support area regeneration.

National urban policy framework

Need for joined-up national regeneration policy

The concern is two-fold. First, while multi-agency integration is required of local partnerships, there remains a chronic lack of joined-up policy reflected in central government's regeneration programmes. In England, for example, there is seen to be a lack of coordination between the DETR, DTI, DfEE, the DoH, the Home Office and the DSS, the latter of which has a vital role in alleviation of poverty. The longevity of this situation is indicated by the fact that a report prepared in 1990 on area regeneration by the lead author of this research took central government to task for poor coordination between the then Department of the Environment and DTI, pointing out chapter and verse where poor coordination hampered local housing-based regeneration (Carley, 1990).

The research revealed concern among regeneration practitioners that, despite the promotion of partnership, there are limitations in central government's policy framework in terms of a failure to achieve a 'joined-up' national policy framework, giving rise to 'zoneitis' locally, and in terms of failure to balance spatial patterns of the country's economic development on a more equitable, rational basis.

Lack of a joined-up approach between different national paymasters can have an important impact on the capacity of partnerships on the ground to respond to local issues and to coordinate initiatives in nearby neighbourhoods. The fact that different partnerships work to different sets of top-down imperatives, from DETR, the Home Office, the DoH, etc, can present barriers to effective local collaboration. Each funding programme will in turn have its own set of bidding criteria, time frame, spatial scale, and required output measures for monitoring.

A key issue on monitoring from the viewpoint of local regeneration practitioners is that central government should recognise that qualitative factors may be as important as quantitative factors in local quality of life. Inappropriate or unsophisticated monitoring requirements intended simply to justify programme expenditure sap resources that might go to devising indicators more relevant to local needs.

There is also concern that the proliferation of small, area-based regeneration programmes and partnerships, such as under SRB, HAZs, Sure Start, New Deal for Communities and so on, called 'zoneitis', is obscuring the need to develop appropriate mechanisms and partnerships for achieving strategic regeneration objectives at the level of the city-region. This would need to be based on a long-term, incremental approach, learning about what works and what does not, and with considerable scope for regional variations in approach and innovation which might lead to success or, sometimes, failure.

Partnership may be necessary to achieve regeneration and social inclusion, but it is unlikely that the establishment of partnerships alone will be sufficient to a difficult task, in which there has still been only limited success. Population decline in northern city-regions continues, as does area abandonment and spatial concentration of disadvantaged households. Partnerships cannot succeed against the grain of national economic and demographic trends.

The situation of coming generations of children and young adults conditions all aspects of regeneration. Because another disadvantaged generation, and one behind *it*, are coming into adulthood, national education policy, and policies that affect families with children, may have a dramatic affect on regeneration and social inclusion – or not, as the case may be.

A national development policy, encompassing linked objectives for urban and rural development and promoting a spatial balance North and South, may be essential to allow regeneration partnerships to achieve major objectives. This would have to link land use and transport with economic development.

Need to buttress partnership efforts in national policy

A related concern of practitioners is that regeneration programmes, however successful, are weakened by limitations in the national policy framework. These are of two sorts. First, there is insufficient devolution of authority and financial control to local authorities to allow them to unlock innovation in their partnerships. Indeed, the top-down (but not joined-up) nature of regeneration programmes, in what have been called 'policy silos', and the 'zoneitis' that is the result, can be seen to reflect the norm of tight centralised control over local partnership activities.

Second, there is felt to be insufficient policy attention to, and strategic investments in, sectors critical to regeneration, particularly education and public transport infrastructure. Government, it is felt, should be promoting overall strategic urban development to underpin regeneration efforts, especially in the formerly industrial cities hard hit by job and population loss.

For England, there is no confidence as yet that the RDAs will fulfil this role, particularly since part of the task may be to direct economic development away from overheated areas to the industrialised, northern city-regions which continue to lose population to the South East, and away from popular rural, greenfield areas to brownfield areas in inner cities. Similarly, high-quality ground transport links between northern cities and Europe may also trigger regeneration (Carley and Kirk, 1999). It is hoped that the forthcoming Urban White Paper will tackle these issues. Interestingly, the first fledgling steps in this direction can be found in the National Development Strategy for Wales, prepared by its European Task Force, a national partnership of 21 organisations. This in turn provides a development context for the Valleys/West Wales SPD.

Timing of funding to partnerships: the cart before the horse?

Many partnerships complain that the pressure of having to spend project-designated money in a particular year, including 'year one' of partnership, can preclude laying the necessary groundwork to build partnership competence and to work towards a mutually agreeable regeneration strategy. Although concern is widespread, the issue is felt particularly strongly by community group partners in regeneration who feel that the timing of bidding and funding almost always reflect bureaucratic imperatives and almost never community aspirations for a steady, incremental approach to building community competence to engage in regeneration.

Given this, it may be appropriate for central funding arrangements to allow an appropriate delay of major funding for 12 to 18 months as necessary to local requirements, with an initial smaller flow of resources directed specifically into partnership building and skills development, community capacity and strategy development.

Central government's partners

In England, New Commitment to Regeneration has been launched by the DETR working with the Local Government Association. This is a potentially powerful model, in that through it agendas of regeneration and local government modernisation could be combined to beneficial effect. The Scottish Executive and the Confederation of Scottish Local Authorities, and the National Assembly for Wales and the Welsh Local Government Association, might profitably explore a similar relationship.

Figure 7: Coherent policy framework

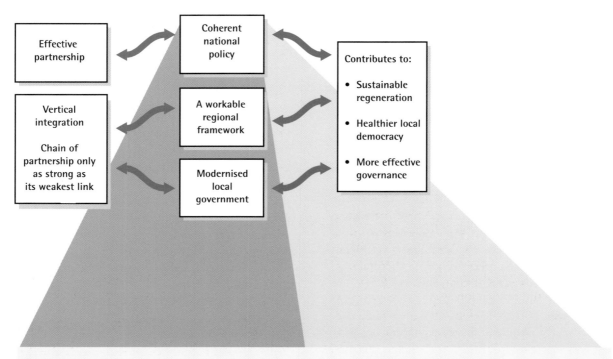

Key points

- Need for a strategic national framework linking urban and rural development

- Need for national investment to support cities, for example, in education and transport

- Important role for government in instigating partnerships

- Need for more joined-up government between policy sectors, such as areas run by the DETR, DTI and DfEE

- Reduction of 'zoneitis' and more coherence in regeneration funding

- Effective pacing of regeneration funding to better suit local requirements

- Enabling monitoring and evaluation reflecting local regeneration requirements

- Transfer of good practice from partnership to partnership

7

Conclusion and recommendations

There is no doubt that the rise of partnership as a means of organising people and resources around the difficult tasks of urban regeneration and social inclusion has been a positive step. There are many examples in this report of good partnership working, and it seems unlikely that single agencies working on their own, even a multi-functional local authority, could have achieved as much without partnership. Furthermore, the approach of joint working between government, business, community and voluntary sector, which defines partnership, is now spreading from the regeneration arena to a more common way of working for better local governance as a whole.

It is likely that the quality of partnerships will continue to improve the longer partnerships are in place. In many cities there is recognition that permanent, rather than solely funding-driven, partnerships are necessary to promote not only regeneration, but sustainable urban development. The lessons of partnership, and of what have been called the foundation stones of partnership, are brought together in Figure 8.

However we should be far from complacent. The tasks of regeneration are getting no easier, in part because we have tackled the easier tasks first, such as physical regeneration near canals and revitalisation of city centres, as in Manchester, Birmingham or Stratford in East London. These are important and impressive projects, vital to broader regeneration objectives and to encouraging changes in perception and thus inward investment. There are also success stories, not only of partnership, but of community-based and neighbourhood regeneration – Greater Pilton in Edinburgh, the Arts Factory in Rhondda, Community Links in Newham and so on.

Despite some success, it is also the case that regeneration in some areas of the city has simply shifted disadvantaged households elsewhere – concentrating them in social housing, both in the council and housing association tenures, and in private rented accommodation. In the worst cases, area abandonment and dereliction continues apace, particularly as population continues to decline in northern industrial cities. Of course cities like Glasgow and Manchester are achieving modest economic success, but there is also evidence that the residents of those cities are not participating in that economic upturn. In Glasgow, for example, although the number of jobs in the city is increasing, the number of jobs in the city held by Glasgow residents is continuing to decline, from 49% in 1998 to an expected 40% in 2006 (Burns, 1999).

In other places, such as Rhondda Cynon Taff, 'third- or fourth-generation' unemployment has become a way of life. On Glasgow's Castlemilk estate, the subject of 10 years of a flagship partnership initiative, only a third of residents are in employment and 80% of employable residents have no educational qualifications. The cycle continues among the next generation – on any one day in Glasgow an estimated 6,000 young people are truant from school, while at the same time fear of disruptive young people 'hanging about' is so strongly perceived that elderly residents are reported to be afraid to leave their house (Pearson, 1999). The quality of the schools themselves are undermined by declining school roles, as households economically able to leave the city for the suburbs continue to do so, increasing the fixed cost of educational establishment per child for families left behind.

Figure 8: An enabling framework for partnership urban regeneration

Contributes to:

- Sustainable regeneration

- Healthier local democracy

- More effective governance

Coherent national policy

- Important role for government in instigating partnership
- Need for more joined-up government between policy sectors, such as run by the DETR, DTI and DfEE
- Reduction of 'zoneitis' and more coherence in Challenge Funding
- Effective pacing of regeneration funding to better suit local requirements
- Enabling of monitoring and evaluation reflecting local regeneration requirements
- Transfer of good practice from partnership to partnership

A workable regional framework

- Need for overall coherent development framework linking economy, regeneration, social inclusion, transport and land use, and sustainability
- In England, clear, complementary functions for Government Offices, RDAs, Regional Assemblies, other regional organisations and (in London) Mayor's Office
- RDAs should support, rather than threaten, sub-regional partnerships
- More organised institutional framework may be needed in areas of unitary local government, especially for Scotland and Wales

Modernised local government

- Visionary council leadership
- Clear corporate approach
- Regeneration within a strong Chief Executive's Department
- Embrace of a modernisation agenda including new positive role for local councillors outside 'cabinet'
- Empowerment of local neighbourhoods on a systematic basis with clear role in community planning and Best Value

Effective partnership

- Strong political and executive leadership at most senior level
- Use of visioning processes as a focal point for consensus building among partners
- Translation of vision into practical objectives for urban development and local regeneration
- Inclusion of key stakeholders in partnership: community, business, police, health authority, education sector, and others
- Effective structure – a balance between inclusiveness and effectiveness
- High quality human resources as the backbone of partnership
- Organisational culture supportive of partnership

Vertical integration: chain of partnership only as strong as its weakest link

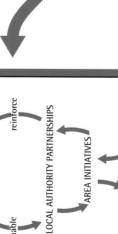

SUB/REGIONAL AND GREATER METROPOLITAN PARTNERSHIPS

reinforce

enable

LOCAL AUTHORITY PARTNERSHIPS

AREA INITIATIVES

NEIGHBOURHOOD/ESTATE PARTNERSHIPS

More generally, partnerships themselves are likely to make little progress against the tide of child poverty in Britain, with 4.3 million children classified as poor. Of these, 2.3 million live in households with no one in work (IFS, 1999).

So there is no cause for complacency. Improvements in partnership, such as funding arrangements and timing that is geared to the task at hand rather than bureaucratic convenience, will need to go hand-in-hand with major steps forward in central government policy and funding, particularly in key areas such as education. For if there is one thing many households in disadvantaged neighbourhoods have in common, it is low literacy and numeracy skills, and low levels of educational attainment. There is ample evidence that the problem is passing into yet another generation of primary school students, with the whole situation made worse by the extent of child poverty and the low levels of aspiration that go with it. In the hi-tech world of the future, with its emphasis on transferable skills in communication, technology and self-management, there are likely to be diminishing opportunities of satisfying employment for the poorly educated.

Recommendations

Broadening the base of partnership

Strong, effective partnerships are built on the meaningful involvement of a full range of key regional and local agencies and organisations. In order for partnerships to develop their strategic capacity, they need to devise plans and programmes that truly integrate the various perspectives, resources and activities of the public, private and third sectors. In particular, effectiveness depends on securing a broad base of participation from the many players who have a hand in local governance and/or substantially influence the quality of life of disadvantaged households. Thus, participation needs to encompass, for example, the health trusts, the Employment Service, the Benefits Agency, the police, housing organisations and associations, schools, colleges, universities and the many voluntary organisations.

More effort also needs to be made to involve the business community – given that only a minority of the partnerships studied here had effective business involvement, and some, even at the city-wide and sub-regional level, had virtually none.

In order to make sure that the expertise and capacities of these agencies are used to the maximum for the benefit of the partnership, it is essential that:

- responsibilities for leadership, agenda setting and management are shared between the partners;

- the 'personality' and culture of the lead partner is not allowed to dominate the partnership;

- space is made for different agencies to participate in their own way and at their own pace;

- agencies consider how appropriate their own structures and cultures are for partnership working, and are prepared to change these in order to become more effective partners.

Genuinely involving the community

A feature of many regeneration areas is the widespread feeling of residents that public agencies have failed them. They feel they have no influence over local authority decision processes, and therefore lack confidence in public agencies as well as in themselves. Despite this, too much community involvement in partnership tends to be tokenistic, that is involving only a few 'community representatives', and/or controlled by public agencies and regeneration professionals where agenda and decision processes are determined with little reference to the wider community.

Phrases like 'community capacity building' are used by public agencies without a full understanding of the processes involved. There is little recognition that community involvement ought to produce a transfer of power to those currently powerless. To work towards this, regeneration programmes should:

- at the beginning, clearly articulate the role expected of the community – both the wider community and representatives – with review and amendment of that role as community confidence increases;

- budget and plan for community development, training and capacity building from the start;

- ensure that the other partners, especially public agencies, understand community development processes;

- be structured in a way that allows strategic objectives to be changed to reflect the views of the wider community;

- devolve budgets and establish locality budgeting mechanisms so that local neighbourhoods and/or areas are genuinely empowered by having a real stake in service planning and quality assessment;

- measure success in terms of community confidence, skills and experience, and residents' views of regeneration achievements.

Addressing the barriers to joined-up action

Statutory agencies, including local authorities, central government and other key public sector organisations, often are bounded by organisational structures, budgets and service delivery requirements rather than by what may be best for deprived areas or for communities in need. As a consequence, regeneration stakeholders have to shift focus from one to another policy and spending 'silo' – which acts as a barrier to joint working.

Joint working requires a degree of power sharing in partnership arrangements and changing organisational cultures, through training and the sharing of best practice, which seeks to stress the benefits of the partnership and not the individual goals of departments or agencies concerned. Removing barriers and obstacles to creating joined-up thinking means moving decision makers out of their policy and organisational silos and making individuals, teams and whole agencies think differently about their own working practices, how this effects partnership working and, ultimately the fortunes of regeneration areas and disadvantaged households. Section III of this report discussed means to joined-up action to support partnership working: a corporate strategy approach in the local authority, a coordinated regional development framework, and better coordination among central government departments and agencies.

Fostering better local governance as an aid to regeneration

This report highlights a potentially important contribution of local government modernisation to partnership regeneration. This view is finding increasing resonance – not least from those local authority officers and politicians who see the benefits of modernisation and have the courage to break with old ways of doing things.

There are many inspiring examples, but also much scope to share inspiration and good practice more effectively. To foster this, each of three countries studied, in their own way, would benefit from establishment of a government-sponsored, but partnership-organised, Modern Local Government Good Practice Unit, to:

• help local authorities re-think their strategic and management role for the 21st century;

• foster and fund innovation in visioning, Best Value, community empowerment, area budgeting and so on;

• address issues of 'democratic deficit' including low voter turnouts and the need to rethink the role of ward councillors;

• link modernisation to regeneration and social inclusion agendas;

• help local authorities learn to work with neighbourhood and community groups as agents of sustainable development, to achieve the Prime Minister's stated goal of "a national strategy for neighbourhood renewal";

• inspire and disseminate good practice.

The Local Government Association for England itself recently posed the question about the need for such an organisation in connection with the Lord Rogers' Urban Task Force report:

Is [there a need for] another commission on local government, charged with answering the big question raised by the Task Force – how can local government reach a fit state to lead an urban renaissance in which, under the less glamorous name of regeneration, it is already so heavily involved? (Pike, 1999)

Just as partnership in 1990 was a positive step, so the modernisation of local government is necessary step on a regeneration journey which, it is clear to many observers, cannot be disentangled from the overarching need for good urban governance. A plus factor is that this research shows that, not only are the agendas of partnership, regeneration, community participation and local governance one and the same, but proposals for the further modernisation of local government are pushing at an open door.

A new financial regime for urban regeneration

Effective regeneration requires an integrated, coordinated approach to funding. Financial inflexibility within a plethora of new initiatives announced by government, often based on the principle of Challenge funding with short time-scales, may not be the most appropriate way to deliver optimum benefits. The competitive bidding process, although with 'catalyst' benefits to kick-start partnership, is time-consuming and resource-intensive and arose in a particular period of central–local government relations. Locally, when a deprived neighbourhood loses out on a challenge bid, frustration and anger is the result, particularly from residents who feel they have been 'led on'. Although there may be a place for specific types of Challenge funding, current arrangements within a myriad of initiatives may not be the best way to build capacity for innovation in tackling the difficult, evolving, challenges of regeneration.

There is insufficient devolution of authority and financial control to local authorities to allow them to unlock innovation in their partnerships, or to define and carry out a strategic role for themselves and partners. Indeed, the top-down (but not joined-up) nature of regeneration programmes, in what have been called 'policy silos', and the 'zoneitis' that is the result, can be seen to reflect the norm of tight centralised control over local partnership activities. The quid pro quo of local government modernisation and the delivery of Best Value should be greater empowerment of local authorities.

There is a need, therefore, for greater flexibility in the use of financial resources. The time is right for all stakeholders, including central government, local authorities and other public and private agencies, to work together towards a more integrated, holistic and innovative approach to the funding of regeneration partnerships. There could be a streamlining of existing regeneration programmes and their merger into a block regeneration grant which would allow for a considerable degree of innovation at the local level. The block grant from central government would be coordinated and carefully monitored at the appropriate regional or city-wide level, such as by the GOR, and implemented through needs-based city-wide and local partnerships.

One approach that ought to be considered for distributing the block grant is the contract model, as in the well known *contrats de ville*, linked to terms of reference for partnerships, whereby city and sub-regional regeneration strategies are developed in negotiation between central and local government and other partners. The contract represents a formal agreement signed by all partners with agreement on strategy coordination, objectives and funding. The regeneration contracts are formally linked into national urban strategies and expenditure programmes.

Within the contract approach, central government funding could do more to foster good practice in the process of partnership development, and in developing the aims and objectives of partnership beyond the usual bland statements that characterise too many strategies. Partnerships could be asked to develop explicit terms of reference which both describe the remit of the partnership and clarify what is expected of each of the partners. Terms of reference would to be subject to negotiation and evolution over time, but they might stipulate:

- the role and remit of the overall partnership, including area of operation, strategic and operational tasks, relationships with other partnerships and key development agencies and so on;

- the intended membership of the partnership, and what is expected of each partner – in terms of strategy development, internal corporate planning objective setting and delivery of outputs;

- a community participation strategy including capacity building;

- proposals for business involvement;

- proposals for team building at steering group, senior management and front-line provider level.

Vertical integration – fostering a chain of sustainable development

This report has stressed the importance of vertical integration – necessary to enhance partnership regeneration at all levels – which means positive, supportive linkage between neighbourhood, city, sub- and regional partnerships. This requirement has been reflected in the cluster approach to the study.

Positive linkage between partnerships and initiatives at various levels is a chain of sustainable development that is *only as strong as its weakest link*. Vertical integration ensures that bottom-up and top-down initiatives form a coherent whole, so that all are pulling in the same direction rather than at cross-purposes. Using the term 'subsidiarity' also implies that decisions are pushed down the chain and taken at the appropriate spatial level, which is why we have called for the empowerment of regions, local authorities and neighbourhood communities with appropriate functions and democratic opportunities.

Just as the growth of partnership has meant better horizontal linkage, so the importance of vertical integration is now being recognised. In particular, the rise of city-wide partnerships, such as those documented here, has been a real achievement of the past few years. These do two things: they promote the economic and social vitality of the city as whole, on a visionary and consensual basis, which then underpins all aspects of regeneration; and they provide a coherent development framework for local efforts, so that regeneration in one neighbourhood is not simply displacing problems to another, and so that positive developments in one area, such as the Commonwealth Stadium in Manchester or Granton foreshore redevelopment in Edinburgh, supports regeneration in adjacent, socially excluded, neighbourhoods. City-wide partnerships need not always be formal, as the informal Chief Executive's Forum in Newham has demonstrated. Another important area of progress has been the rise of sub-regional and regional partnerships, such as Thames Gateway or South Yorkshire Forum, which provide a similar positive relationship with city-level, and thus local, partnerships.

This trend to vertical integration requires continued support. Political and funding structures should assist the establishment of partnerships at levels where they are needed but don't yet exist – some neighbourhood partnerships in adjacent local authorities, city-wide partnerships, which ought to exist almost everywhere, and sub- and regional partnerships. Care should be taken to ensure that efforts are complementary so that, for example, RDA-based partnerships don't undermine existing sub-regional partnerships organised around travel-to-work areas. It is also important for Scotland and Wales to question whether new partnerships need to be developed or strengthened, such as between Glasgow, Edinburgh and other nearby urban areas such as north Lanarkshire, or in the Welsh Valleys. Finally, organisational culture in key agencies should encourage and reward both partnership working (often not the case) and vertical integration (seldom as yet seen as a worthwhile task, but looming on the horizon as a key aspect of regeneration activity).

Supportive regional development frameworks

Beyond the linkage between partnerships at various spatial levels, a regional development framework could be essential to underpin efforts at urban regeneration. A comparison of British and continental European experience suggests the benefits of a regional perspective (Carley and Kirk, 1999).

This form of regional development is about more than economic or business development, although that is important. It also links economic advancement with objectives for social inclusion, so that disadvantaged households and neighbourhoods benefit from inward investments and new opportunities for employment, and with objectives for improving quality of life and health, so that economic development is not at the expense of the environment.

Each of the United Kingdom's constituent countries will devise regional frameworks suited to its needs. For England, the key issue is to ensure complementarity between activities and funding mechanisms of Government Offices for the Regions, RDAs, Regional Assemblies and other regional organisations. At present just the fact that such organisations are coming into being and getting to work on regional issues is a plus factor. But soon there could be a plethora of regional agencies – and benefits will be maximised only if there is a substantial degree of coordination.

There need not be a national model – each region could work towards consensual arrangements, but national guidance on key factors to take into account would be helpful. This report suggests strategic analysis, forward planning and mediation between local authorities over difficult development decisions, leavened with a measure of democratic accountability, however devised. There also needs to be a framework for coordinating regeneration strategy, labour market analysis, inward investment, transport and land use planning and sustainability objectives, such as for reducing CO_2 emissions and directing new development towards decontaminated, brownfield sites well served by public transport. All this is done most effectively at a regional level.

For Scotland and Wales, local government reorganisation has left something of a regional vacuum, which affects the viability of regeneration at the city and local levels. There are, of course, many good partnerships and real progress at the city-wide and SIP level, particularly with Partnership Support funding. But the question has to be asked whether the flow of benefits from regeneration funding is maximised in the absence of a more formal regional framework. A vacuum is there to be filled, and both countries have the chance for real organisational and political innovation at the regional level.

A national development policy promoting urban and rural areas

At first glance it may seem odd to conclude a report on urban regeneration partnerships with mention of rural development, but it is the case that, in a small, densely settled country, the health of urban and rural areas is closely intertwined. The research revealed concern among regeneration practitioners that, despite promotion of partnership, there are limitations in central government's policy framework in terms of failure to balance spatial patterns of the country's economic development on a more equitable, rational basis. Government, it is felt, should be promoting overall strategic urban development to underpin regeneration efforts, especially in the formerly industrial cities hard hit by job and population loss. There is felt to be insufficient policy attention to, and strategic investments in, sectors critical to regeneration, particularly education and public transport infrastructure. For example, high speed rail with integrated ground transport between Britain's northern cities and continental Europe may trigger regeneration, as it is doing in Spain, France, the Netherlands and so on.

Part of the task may be to direct economic development away from overheated areas to the industrialised, northern city-regions which continue to lose population to the South East, and away from popular rural, market town and greenfield areas to brownfield areas in inner cities. The forthcoming Urban White Paper should tackle these issues. Interestingly, the first fledgling steps in this direction can be found in the National Development Strategy for Wales, prepared by its European Task Force, a national partnership of 21 organisations.

In short, a national development policy, or settlement strategy, encompassing linked objectives for urban and rural development, and promoting a spatial balance between North and South, may be essential to allow regeneration partnerships at all levels to achieve major objectives. This would have to link land use and transport with economic development and objectives for achieving sustainable development and quality of life.

References

Burns, M. (1999) Presentation from Castlemilk Economic Development Agency to the Scottish Urban Regeneration Forum, November.

Carley, M. (1990) *Housing and neighbourhood renewal: Britain's new urban challenge*, London: Policy Studies Institute.

Carley, M. (1997) *Waterfront development and urban regeneration in North Edinburgh: Assessment of key issues*, Edinburgh: Scottish Homes, Lothian, Borders and Forth Valley Region.

Carley, M. and Christie, I. (1992) *Managing sustainable development*, London: Earthscan/ Kogan Page.

Carley, M. and Kirk, K. (1998) *Sustainable by 2020? A strategic approach to urban regeneration in Britain's cities*, Bristol: The Policy Press.

Carley, M. and Kirk, K. (1999) *City-wide urban regeneration: Lessons from good practice*, Edinburgh: Central Research Unit, Scottish Executive.

Community Links (1999) *Social Enterprise Zone Update 3*, October.

Dean, J., Hastings, A., More, A. and Young, R. (1999) *Fitting together? A study of partnership processes in Scotland*, Edinburgh: Scottish Homes.

IFS (Institute for Fiscal Studies) (1999) *Poor kids: Trends in child poverty in Britain 1968-96*, London: IFS.

London Borough of Newham, (1999) *Report to the Best Value Sub Committee – Defining and delivering Best Value – regeneration*, 13 July, London: Partnerships and Regeneration Division, Chief Executive's Office, London Borough of Newham.

New Start (1999) 'Huge renewal plan for East Manchester', 5 November.

Pearson, G. (1999) Presentation from the Assistant Chief Constable of Strathclyde Police to the Scottish Urban Regeneration Forum, November.

Pike, A. (1999) 'Is Rogers' renaissance any different from regeneration?', *Local Government Talkback*, Local Government Association, July.

Robinson, D., Dunn, K. and Ballintyne, S. (1998) *Social Enterprise Zones: Bringing innovation into regeneration*, York: York Publishing Services.

Scottish Executive (1999) *Social justice ... a Scotland where everyone matters*, Edinburgh: Scottish Executive.

Scottish Social Inclusion Network (1999) *Report of the Strategy Action Team*, Edinburgh: Scottish Executive.

SEU (Social Exclusion Unit) (1998) *Bringing Britain together: A national strategy for neighbourhood renewal*, Cm 4045, London: The Stationery Office.

Turok, I. and Edge, N. (1999) *The jobs gap in Britain's cities: Employment loss and labour market consequence*, Bristol: The Policy Press.

University of Glasgow (1999) *Edinburgh and Glasgow: Contrasts in competitiveness and cohesion*, Glasgow: Department of Urban Studies, University of Glasgow.

Urban Task Force (1999) *Towards an urban renaissance*, London: E and FN Spon.

Wales, R. and Mcauley, C. (1998) *Newham: Maintaining the momentum*.

Appendix: The case studies

England

East London
- Thames Gateway Partnership
- Newham Chief Executive's Forum
- Forest Gate and Plaistow Sustainable Communities Initiative

Greater Manchester
- Manchester City Pride
- Salford Partnership
- Cheetham and Broughton Partnership

Birmingham
- Birmingham City Pride
- Birmingham Economic Development Partnership
- Handsworth Community Safety Partnership

Middlesbrough/Tees Valley
- Tees Valley Joint Strategy Unit
- Middlesbrough Direct City-wide Partnership
- Grove Hill 2000

Sheffield
- South Yorkshire Forum
- Sheffield First Partnership
- Netherthorpe and Upperthorpe Community Alliance

Wales

The Valleys/Rhondda Cynon Taff
- Valleys Partnership
- Rhondda Cynon Taff
- Arts Factory Ferndale

Scotland

Glasgow
- Glasgow Alliance
- Gorbals Partnership
- Crown Street Regeneration Project

Edinburgh
- Capital City Partnership
- North Edinburgh Area Renewal Project
- Pilton Partnership

North Lanarkshire
- Lanarkshire Alliance
- North Lanarkshire Partnership
- Motherwell North Social Inclusion Partnership

England

East London

The densely populated 10 boroughs of East London are historically associated with light and heavy industry and the docklands along the River Thames. Industrial decline means that there are many large tracts of developable land, and significant social exclusion remains a challenge, despite many years of what has been described as 'industrial gentrification' by the London Docklands Development Corporation.

In the centre of East London, the London Borough of Newham, in the words of residents' organisation Community Links, "has experienced every state-sponsored regeneration initiative since the 1960s ... with examples of all current initiatives within walking distance". Initiatives include designation as a New Commitment to Regeneration Pathfinder, New Deal for Community, Education and Health Action Zones and 23 SRB projects.

Newham is one of England's most deprived boroughs, but it also contains many vibrant communities with a strong sense of place, each with a distinguishable high street as the focus of daily life. It is ethnically diverse, with some neighbourhoods having a majority of Asian and Afro-Caribbean residents. Newham's regeneration involves many physical projects, such as the new campus of East London University at City Airport, and the extended Jubilee Line with three architecturally significant new tube–bus interchanges within the borough. But the challenges of multiple deprivation remain acute both on council estates and in private housing, and the council is concerned that the borough is too often perceived as "a transit camp where people stay as long as they have to, and then move out at the first available opportunity, while those who cannot afford to move reluctantly stay, dreaming of a move elsewhere" (Wales and Mcauley, 1998).

There are many partnerships. The research project looked at the **Thames Gateway Partnership**, founded in 1995 to develop strategic vision for East London, north and south of the Thames, as an economic and social region, and linking 12 local authorities; the Newham **Chief Executive's Forum** which brings together representatives of key agencies; and, at the local level, the **Forest Gate and Plaistow Sustainable Communities Initiative**. We also looked at the 10-year-old East London Partnership of business organisations.

East London's partnerships: key issues

- *Valuable sub-regional partnership:* The Thames Gateway Partnership (TGP) is a sub-regional partnership said to link, for the first time, 12 local authorities north and south of the river in London and Kent in a common economic and human resources agenda – as an economic sub-region with strong transport links to the rest of Europe. The partnership is seen as a "bridge between local authorities and government", receiving additional political support from an all-party Parliamentary group of local MPs. TGP roles are: partnership building, coordination of policy and services such as a sub-regional framework for skills strategies, lobbying, advisory services, skills development in partnership working, area promotion and marketing. Its board is made up of key politicians from the constituent local authorities. To link with local initiative, TGP supports a community network of nearly 400 organisations.

- *Local authority backing for modernisation and partnership:* The evolving approach of the London Borough of Newham to partnership is a key to success from the viewpoint of its partners. Achievements in regeneration and partnership are supported by three factors: full commitment of the leader and chief executive to a modernisation agenda, including Vision 2010, a Chief Executive's Forum (CEF), and a strong, well staffed Regeneration and Partnerships Division answering directly to the chief executive.

- *Chief Executive's Forum:* The CEF includes a full range of stakeholders including community representatives, health board, police and business and is viewed by member agencies as valuable means of communication and joint working. The CEF is serviced by the Chief Executive's Department. The police, for example, credit the forum with providing the means for them to work in an integrated manner with local authority, health authority, community groups and schools to improve public safety. For the police, this included a highly successful 'listening day' with local residents and schools organised under the auspices of the council leader's Newham 2010 initiative. Overall, the CEF is rated by stakeholders as an effective model. However, there is concern that, not being formal, it is dependent for its continued effectiveness on the commitment of the current chief executive, and may be at risk when the chief executive changes.

- *Social Enterprise Zone:* The Forest Gate Plaistow Sustainable Communities regeneration partnership is seeking to extend the local partnership approach by designating it as a Social Enterprise Zone. This seeks to make partnership regeneration more relevant by bending mainstream policy and expenditure to tackle deprivation – by identifying statutory laws and rules that could be altered to achieve local benefits and by creative involvement of local residents in long-term regeneration programmes.

- *Community Forums:* At the borough level, to supplement partnership participation, local planning is being organised around six Community Forums which are charged with preparing a local plan addressing key issues and securing commitment from agencies for a joint approach to implementation. Issues of neighbourhood democracy and partnership are discussed in Chapters 3 and 5.

Greater Manchester

Greater Manchester conurbation comprises 10 local authorities. It is often described as a rather balkanised entity, with strong local identities in the towns that surround the regional centre in Manchester, and a persistent rivalry between the two cities at the heart of the conurbation, Manchester and Salford. Despite this, there are a few governance mechanisms that arch over the conurbation, the most significant of which is the Association of Greater Manchester Authorities, an inter-authority alliance of the 10.

Since 1994, the three local authorities in the core conurbation – Manchester, Salford, and Trafford – have been part of Manchester City Pride, a partnership which has focused attention on the most disadvantaged areas within the conurbation. In 1997 the three founding members of the partnership were joined by Tameside MBC. Led by Manchester City Council, the partnership brings together four very different local authorities and a wide range of public, private and voluntary sector partnerships around a broad urban development agenda.

As a key example of a sub-regional partnership, City Pride forms the top level of the Greater Manchester case study. The case study also includes the Salford Partnership, which was formed in 1995 as a bid to the first round of SRB, and is a local authority-wide partnership with a thematic focus, although it also acts as an umbrella for area-based regeneration schemes. At the time of the research, it had recently been awarded 'pathfinder' status under the New Commitment to Regeneration initiative, and a review of the partnership was underway. The local level partnership in the case study is the Cheetham and Broughton Partnership, a joint initiative of Manchester and Salford City Councils as part of SRB round 2. This was the first two-council SRB, and the 'partnership' is in reality joint working between two councils that have different cultures and approaches. Its importance lies in the fact that there are likely to be more regeneration areas that straddle administrative boundaries.

Greater Manchester's partnerships: key issues

- Manchester City Pride was established as a mechanism for involving a broad range of partners in developing a shared common agenda and vision for the core of the conurbation. Led by Manchester City Council, it brought to the table for the first time four local authorities with almost no track record in collaboration, along with the key public agencies operating within and across the sub-region, private sector interests and, more recently, voluntary sector organisations. It has clearly been a useful vehicle for developing dialogue among a broad church of partners. Two strategy documents produced under City Pride have provided reference points for the activities of individual partners, raised the profile of the core conurbation with central and regional government, and added weight to bids for resources for regeneration.

- However, it has become apparent that, while City Pride has been a useful vehicle for a developing a sub-regional vision as well as relationships between partners, a rather different partnership approach might be required in order for strategic thinking and joined-up action to be achieved, particularly in relation to partners' mainstream programmes and services. External pressures, such as local government modernisation and Best Value, interacting with internal pressures for a more inclusive approach to partnership, mean that City Pride is currently going through a transitional phase in which its future role and nature are being questioned. The evidence is that this questioning phase could be productive to the rethinking of the objectives and operation of the partnership.

- Within the context of City Pride, the Salford Partnership, set up in 1995, is the first local authority-wide, strategic partnership involving the key players to be established in that city. Formed as a thematic bid to the first round of SRB, it is an example of how SRB can provide the impetus to develop a broadly based strategic forum capable of taking a city-wide perspective on regeneration. The partnership has since secured 'pathfinder' status under the New Commitment to Regeneration initiative, seen as "a way of reinvigorating and strengthening the partnership", through causing participants to reconsider the role of the partnership and how their mainstream activities have a bearing on regeneration and development. Thus, like City Pride, the Salford Partnership is engaged in a review both of its rationale and its activities. This issue of periodic review seems a vital step in growth and development of partnership, discussed again in Chapter 3.

- Within the case study cluster, there are no formal mechanisms by which dialogue is achieved between local partnerships and city and sub-regional partnerships. This is suggested "not to matter because the fit between the local and strategic partnerships is clear", and in any case is mitigated by overlaps of personnel. However, there may be a missed opportunity in the sub-region for mutual learning between local and strategic initiatives. The question of fit between partnerships is taken up in Chapter 4.

- The Cheetham and Broughton Partnership (CBP) is a joint SRB initiative between two of the local authorities in City Pride, Manchester and Salford, with Manchester TEC and the Greater Manchester Police. CBP illustrates the challenges involved in developing partnership across local authority boundaries. Ideally these difficulties should be addressed early in the life of a partnership, through a focus on developing joint understanding of the culture that operates within the individual authorities, their decision-making processes and their approach to community capacity building and regeneration strategy. Developing joint ownership of the regeneration processes takes time but is essential if the partnership is not to fracture into two or more sub-partnerships and if the added benefits of cross-border working are to be achieved.

Birmingham

Birmingham has a long tradition of civic leadership – under Chamberlain, the city became a model for modern local government. Civic leadership has also played a key role in the way the city has harnessed the expertise and know-how of the private sector on flagship regeneration projects including the National Exhibition Centre and, more recently, Millennium Point. Partnership working, competitiveness, a long-term approach to regeneration and social exclusion and a more participative democracy are current themes which are a continuation of this emphasis on civic leadership.

Birmingham is a diverse city, with a multi-faith population from many ethnic backgrounds. There are areas of affluence alongside areas of extreme poverty, giving a real challenge to regeneration. Birmingham is the fifth most deprived out of 366 districts on the English deprivation index, with 25 of its 39 wards ranked in the most disadvantaged 10% in the country. Ensuring that city-wide and local partnerships act in a concerted manner is seen as important to help deprived communities break out of the cycle of deprivation and social exclusion.

The study analysed three partnerships. City Pride is a city-wide partnership with responsibility for the development and monitoring of a strategic vision for the city. The Birmingham Economic Development Partnership is a multi-agency delivery partnership focused specifically on the economy. At the neighbourhood level, the research team studied the Handsworth Community Safety Project, part of a SRB round 4 scheme, Community Safety in Birmingham.

Birmingham's partnerships: key issues

- New political leadership in the city council has been seen to be very proactive towards partnership working and local government modernisation, instigating the establishment of all-party Public Policy Review Panels and a cabinet-style decision structure. A Democracy Commission has also been established to consult with the city's residents on a range of issues, including the possibility of an elected mayor for the city.

- Birmingham City Pride partnership has been established for five years. It has recently reviewed its own structure and method of operation. One result is that its board has been reconstituted to ensure that it represents a group of senior decision makers who have the authority in board meetings to commit their organisations to action. The board has a chair, independent of its partner members, and a City Pride manager provides support to the board. City Pride is self-funding, with costs met from a joint budget to which all partners contribute.

- Birmingham has a long, solid history of public–private partnership. The Birmingham Economic Development Partnership (BEDP) is a company limited by guarantee and represents the joint interests of the city council, the local Training and Enterprise Company (TEC) and the Chamber of Commerce and Industry. The partnership has taken a pragmatic approach towards providing a single, customer-focused gateway to business support services throughout the city. A key driver of partnership has been the desire to avoid duplication and improve service delivery. Each partner takes lead responsibility for some key partnership activities. Partners have agreed to set in motion a strategy of 'co-location' of workers by which staff can rotate to the partner agencies as required for efficiency.

- Community Safety is an issue of concern for the city. The Birmingham Community Safety Partnership (BCSP) was established under the 1998 Crime and Disorder Act with the aim of developing and implementing a crime reduction strategy for the city. At the local level, Community Safety in Birmingham is a SRB round 4 programme which aims to empower local communities and reduce the obstacles to the economic and social regeneration arising from crime and the fear of crime. One scheme operates in the Handsworth area of the city, a multi-ethnic neighbourhood that was the scene of urban riots in the early 1980s. A problem for the area concerns the fragmented nature of the local community. Community safety is a common theme used to unite community groups and provide a base for crime prevention measures, youth work and addressing the vexed problem of school exclusions.

Middlesbrough and the Tees Valley

Middlesbrough lies in the commercial and retail heart of the Tees Valley but, as in many other areas in the North East, the regional economy and the city have suffered from rounds of deindustrialisation. According to the Index of Local Deprivation, almost one third of Middlesbrough's residents live in deprived wards. However, change is underway – Middlesbrough now has a thriving town centre and a successful, expanding higher and further education sector. Planned health, commercial and retail developments are intended to enhance the town's position and underpin aspirations to city status.

A key strength is the way in which Middlesbrough has approached partnership. Almost every inch of Middlesbrough is now covered by a partnership initiative including an Education Action Zone, Employment Zone, New Deal for Communities and Health Action Zone, plus a range of area-based initiatives in which local people, the council, voluntary groups and businesses work together. Modernisation of decision making and service delivery is another key feature of the council's approach.

The study examined three partnerships: the Tees Valley Joint Strategy Unit (TVJSU), a joint local authority partnership aimed at sub-regional planning and strategic development, Middlesbrough Direct, a new city-wide partnership; and, at the local level, Grove Hill 2000, a community regeneration partnership.

Partnerships in the Tees Valley and Middlesbrough: key issues

- TVJSU was established by the five local authorities of the Tees Valley to provide a strategic development framework for planning, transportation and economic development, and intelligence for the local authorities. TVJSU has 25 board members, representing the local authorities, a staff of 40 and a budget of £1.2 million. The partners recognised that the quality of life for people in the Tees Valley could be enhanced by producing sub-regional strategies which aim to maintain existing jobs and create new employment with the context of sustainable development. A key aim is to ensure that Regional Planning Guidance is in accord with the Regional Economic Strategy.

- Middlesbrough Direct was formed to define a vision for the city, establish a regeneration strategy and coordinate bidding. Links are being forged between the city-wide partnership and the council's new corporate structure including its community-based plans. The driver behind the establishment of Middlesbrough Direct was a successful attempt to secure LGA Pathfinder designation, demonstrating the positive role played by such national programmes.

- A key task as seen by the council involves responding to the modernisation agenda by improving local service delivery. The council has identified two key challenges which define the agenda: democratic renewal, with emphasis on the need for residents to have a say in shaping council policy and decisions, and Best Value. In response, the council has adopted cabinet decision making with 'commissioners' being allocated responsibility for key strategic policy areas. The council also reviewed its management structure, creating four corporate director posts.

- As part of modernisation, Middlesbrough's network of 26 community councils are being reviewed. Creation of new Local Partnership Forums have been suggested as an alternative mechanism to promote community leadership.

Sheffield

Since 1975 Sheffield has lost 80,000 jobs, or a quarter of its manufacturing employment. A radical city administration in the 1980s attempted to prop up the economy with a high-spending, high-rates strategy, leading to palpable tension between local government and the business community. This legacy needed to be overcome before a genuine partnership approach to regeneration could begin to be established.

The late 1980s marked a change in approach. The reorientation of national policy towards private sector involvement coincided with a change in the political complexion of the council and a pragmatic recognition of the limits of radical intervention. This laid the foundation for the current partnership approach between public and private sectors.

In 1991 relations between the private sector and the council had improved, resulting in the formation of the City Liaison Group, forerunner of the current Sheffield First city-wide partnership. However, subsequent failure to secure City Challenge funding is said to have led to recognition that 'cobbled-together partnerships' do not work. Since then Sheffield has been successful in each SRB round, attracting significant levels of investment. This success is attributed to improved partnership working, and better relationship between local and central government, another form of partnership. However, despite recent attempts at economic diversification there has been less success in reducing polarisation between rich and poor residents with many of the city's neighbourhoods qualifying as priority areas. It is now recognised though that the long haul of reversing deep-seated economic trends will only be achieved through effective partnership working at a strategic, as well as local, level.

This is reflected in the range of partnerships. Research focused on the South Yorkshire Forum, a sub-regional partnership responsible for drafting the Objective 1 Single Programming Document (SPD); Sheffield First; and locally, the Netherthorpe and Upperthorpe Community Alliance, an SRB 1 area. Evolving partnership approaches at a regional level were also studied including the Yorkshire and Humberside Assembly and Chamber and Yorkshire Forward, the new RDA.

Sheffield's partnerships: key lessons

- The South Yorkshire Forum (SYF) builds on an earlier initiative, Invest in South Yorkshire, an attempt by the TECs to promote a sub-regional perspective. However, it was Objective 1 designation that sharpened interest in a sub-regional initiative, given concern that, without a strategic approach, matched funding opportunities would ebb away. The Objective 1 designation persuaded neighbouring local authorities to put aside traditional rivalries and develop a collective sense of purpose with Sheffield City. Membership of the Forum has rapidly expanded, but there is a still concern that it is too public sector-dominated. Like many partnerships, effective private sector representation is essential to develop more sophisticated strategy and implementation. Involvement of the private sector in partnership is discussed in Chapter 5.

- Sheffield First is an overarching city-wide partnership, with vision centred around 4 'E's': education, enterprise, equity and excellence. It builds on a failed City Liaison Group which "failed to deliver". Partnership is now seen to have moved from a council-dominated structure to an arrangement of equals, and this shift is said to have revitalised partnership working. Sheffield First sees itself as having a 'brokerage' role in backing bids led by individual partners. Its strategic framework is intended to be reflected within partners' own organisational agendas. There is concern, however, that the city-wide partnership is not linked sufficiently to local partnership action, but "floats above the city without being anchored down". The issue of linkage between levels of partnership is discussed in Chapter 6.

- Sheffield City Council has embraced the modernisation agenda, seeing itself moving towards a 'corporate management' approach. A new chief executive has been instrumental, with five directors as a corporate team looking at council business as a whole and driving forward key priorities. For officers involved in regeneration partnerships at all levels, the new organisational culture fostered by the chief executive is said to have made a "big difference", leading to a departure from "traditional council suspicion of partnership working" toward "real and very positive changes in attitudes". Similarly, the modernising approach has not always filtered down to officers working at a local level. Residents talk of "low staff moral" and have a perception that "people with ambition go off", leaving a residual of officers who are "not best quality, are defensive and lack optimism, which rubs off" on residents.

- The North West Inner City area won funding from the first SRB round. Early attempts to set up a Community Forum were not adequately supported by the council which exacerbated tensions with local residents. Subsequent designation under URBAN is said to have acted as the catalyst for better relations through the establishment of a new Community Alliance (CA) as the driving force in a partnership group of half agency and half community representatives to enable local decision making on grants. A proposed redevelopment with the health authority of a former baths/library into a Healthy Living Centre is an example of the CA's proactive, bottom-up approach to partnership, working with a range of agencies on specific initiatives.

Wales

A Welsh case study was required to complete the three-country perspective. The National Assembly for Wales suggested that the designation of Objective 1 status for the former coalmining area of the Welsh Valleys, and an intense round of strategic planning and partnership activity around this would make a good case study. Investment in the area under Objective 1 could total £1.3 billion during the period 2000-06, giving a vital but short-lived opportunity to 'turn around' the Valleys and sow the seeds of sustainable regeneration.

The Valleys/Rhondda Cynon Taff

The densely settled valleys, containing one quarter of the population of Wales, run north and south from the prosperous M4 corridor. The Valleys are well known as the former premier coalfields of the British empire. Of the Valleys, perhaps the busiest was the Rhondda Valley, which at its peak in 1919 had 41,000 miners working 53 pits, and supporting a population of 163,000 people. By 1934, however, the Rhondda was already in decline and had Special Area status. Now only a single, cooperative deep mine remains of this huge industry. But the Valleys still contain many lively local communities. The reclamation or 'greening' of the blackened, damaged hillsides has been successfully accomplished, giving the area an attractive semi-rural aspect.

Some new manufacturing industry has been attracted, but it is said that not many 'Valley boys' (or girls) work there. Rather, "educated people drive in from outside". Persistently high levels of 'third- or fourth-generation' unemployment mean related social problems including low self-esteem, low levels of literacy and numeracy and a lack of confidence (or desire) to travel out of the Valleys to seek employment. These present real challenges to regeneration. There is said to be a "long history of failed initiatives" and, for many observers, "an over-reliance on capital projects which have not helped disadvantaged residents". Despite obvious problems, residents are very attached to the Valleys and there is strong community spirit in the villages.

The study looked at the Valleys Partnership, a regional partnership covering the entire Valleys Objective 1 area of nine local authorities. The partnership has 'regional facilitators' appointed from two local authorities, and a broad membership. Within this context, regeneration activity was studied in the local authority Rhondda Cynon Taff (RCT) and local regeneration initiatives in the village of Ferndale, whose pit closed in 1959.

The Valleys' partnerships: key issues

- Objective 1 status has been the catalyst for the establishment of the Valleys Partnership. This meant that the new partnership almost immediately came under pressure to prepare a 'regional assessment', leading to a Valleys/West Wales SPD which, in the absence of any other strategic, regional development plan, must fulfil that role if the short-lived opportunity of massive ERDF funding is to be used to maximum long-term benefit in turning around a region much damaged by deindustrialisation. Needing to get 'stuck in' quickly to SPD preparation means that the partnership has not had time to break away from a traditional mode described as being "public sector top-heavy" to include, for example, business and long-standing community groups within the planning process.

- At this regional level, despite the existence of partnership and a 'regional assessment', some mediation mechanism is seen to be required to assess implicit, competing development agendas: between environment/tourism and industrial development/road infrastructure, between strategic and community objectives, between easy car-borne access to new employment and the needs of the many local car-less households, and between capital-intensive physical investment and needs for training and education. As in Scotland, local government reorganisation which imposed a single tier has left what is described as "a strategic vacuum" across the nine city and borough councils in the Valleys, a situation exacerbated by the strong north–south orientation of Valleys transport links. The smaller local authorities created by local government reform are said to be "parochial, with no history of working together". Senior officials in RCT feel that regeneration is hampered by the lack of a physical development strategy for the region as a whole, with the result that some valleys are prospering considerably more than others.

- At this regional level there is also concern about a lack of coherence in visioning and planning. Current approaches are described as "scatter-gun", with "no clarity at a regional level and about 20 different economic strategies", a "lack of vision and targeted policies" with "no leadership on the bigger issues, unwillingness to criticise past development policies and no plans for monitoring the cost-effectiveness of investment". The importance of a regional development framework to underpin sub-regional partnership efforts is discussed in Chapter 8.

- Some respondents find there is lack of clarity over the respective roles of the Valleys Partnership, the Valleys Forum (launched by a Welsh industry minister in 1998) and proposed regional committees of the Welsh Assembly. The biggest risk is that poor partnership organisation and lack of visionary strategic planning will mean reduced benefits flowing from the £1.3 billion investment of Objective 1 monies. The Government Offices of National Assembly for Wales are said to work in an 'a-spatial' manner, with insufficient detailed geographic knowledge.

- There may also be what is described as 'institutional conservatism' in the organisational culture of the offices of the National Assembly for Wales, which inhibits questioning the effectiveness of past approaches to Valleys development, and failure as yet to take a mantle of leadership at the level of the Valleys – given there is no other organisation likely to do so. Leadership is seen as necessary to "manage expectations" and "to establish an intellectual rigour over what are too many pet schemes". On the plus side, there is a new Welsh National Development Strategy, with needs analysis sectorally and regionally. However, it is described by a senior local government member of the Valleys Partnership as "anodyne and therefore not very helpful".

- At the local level, RCT District Council is moving ahead quickly on an agenda of local government modernisation, including a corporate development framework. A recent change in ruling party and wholesale turnover of councillors has reinforced this opportunity, which is contributing to an optimistic climate for partnership.

- The strong sense of community in the Valley is reflected in active community organisations with a strong sense of purpose and an impressive record of practical achievement. These include Blaenllechau Community Regeneration and the Arts Factory Community Development Trust in Ferndale, discussed in Chapter 5.

Scotland

Glasgow

Glasgow's formidable physical, economic and social problems need little introduction. Despite efforts over the past two decades to reinvent Glasgow as a post-industrial 'City of Culture', as well as significant investment in infrastructure and neighbourhood regeneration, large swathes of the city remain home to disadvantaged people, marginalised from economic opportunities, living in neighbourhoods requiring substantial investment.

Glasgow has a long track record in establishing partnerships focused on regeneration issues emerging at different spatial scales, certainly compared with many UK cities. With the launch of each new regeneration programme, Glasgow usually produces a number of neighbourhoods as candidates for initiative status. Consequently, there were a large number of partnerships to choose between as case studies. The research focused on three partnerships as follows.

The Glasgow Alliance, first formally established in 1993, is the key city-wide partnership in the city. Relaunched in 1998, its initial focus on area regeneration has widened to more of a city development remit recently. Over the period it has tended to involve mainly public sector agencies operating within the city, although with its relaunch membership was extended to the Scottish Executive, and securing the effective participation of voluntary and private sector organisations has become more of a priority. The Gorbals Regeneration Partnership is again a mainly public sector alliance, formed in 1986 to oversee the development of this historically deprived area of the city. It was formally constituted as a Social Inclusion Partnership in 1999. The Crown Street Regeneration Project dates from 1990 and is a vehicle for delivering the wholesale redevelopment of one neighbourhood in the Gorbals, involving public sector agencies alongside community representatives.

Glasgow's partnerships: key issues

- The Glasgow Alliance is a renamed, reformed version of an earlier attempt at a city-wide strategic regeneration partnership in the city. Its relaunch in 1998 was designed to deal with what many perceived as a lack of progress, both in developing a clear strategy and in impacting on the ground. The new model seeks to overcome earlier problems by establishing a separate company operating at arm's length from all individual partners, staffed by a dedicated team. A restructuring exercise was conducted to clarify responsibilities for strategy and for operational activity, and the need to provide both vision and a means of implementing it was reflected in the early publication of *Creating tomorrow's Glasgow*. In this strategy document, the vision is backed by five 'headline targets' with action plans and time-scales attached.

- For some, the Glasgow Alliance has signalled a shift of focus with the publication of the new strategy: from 'need' to 'opportunity'. Certainly, compared with its previous two strategies, there is less of an emphasis on priority areas and regeneration in the new strategy, and more of an emphasis on city development and 'social inclusion' for specific generational and social groups. This may represent a broader perspective than hitherto on how to achieve regeneration, and is matched by an explicit recognition that mainstream resources are integral to achieving city regeneration.

- Prior to its relaunch, the Glasgow Alliance was widely criticised for its lack of connection to and engagement with area and neighbourhood partnerships. With the advent of a dedicated staff team, attempts have been made to improve communication and integration between the city-wide strategic partnership and local partnerships. For example, local partnership managers, employed by the Alliance, have been recruited not only to manage the local partnership but also to help mange the relationship between the local and city partnership. An early initiative was to ensure the participation of a senior Alliance staff member in some local partnerships in order to facilitate information exchange. Such developments are a significant step towards integrating local regeneration activity into a city strategic framework.

- The Gorbals Regeneration Partnership has evolved over 14 years as an attempt to coordinate and add value to the activities of an increasing range of agencies involved in developing and providing services in the Gorbals. Until its designation as a formal Social Inclusion Partnership (SIP) in 1999, it probably lacked presence and appears to have struggled to maintain an identity and profile with decision takers in the partner organisations. Despite the annual publication of a strategy document, without the explicit commitment of partners to this agenda, it proved impossible to fashion a strategic approach to regeneration. It is expected that SIP status may help to change this situation.

- By contrast, there has been strong commitment from key players in the city to the Crown Street Regeneration Project which is redeveloping a large site in the Gorbals area. This partnership has benefited from the high-profile sustained involvement of senior officers from a small number of partners with the capacity to influence the priorities and expenditure of partners. Again, in contrast to the larger Gorbals Partnership, Crown Street has also benefited from resources being provided for dedicated staff, local premises, and strong leadership from the top of one of the partner organisations.

Edinburgh

One of the UK's most affluent cities, Edinburgh enjoys a buoyant if not booming economy. The main challenge for city governance and partnership is therefore to manage growth rather than decline, and to try to include the city's larger public sector housing estates, characterised by problems of poverty and physical decline, in the city's prosperity. Since the late 1980s, a series of local area regeneration initiatives have been established, although a strategic approach to regeneration across the city was not developed until 1995 with the formation of Edinburgh Capital City Partnership. There are a multitude of inter-agency partnerships currently in operation concerned with different aspects of the city's development, such as culture or 'lifelong learning'. In late 1998, a new partnership – the Edinburgh Partnership Group – was established as an overarching mechanism for all of this activity, with a remit to produce a community plan for the city.

The Edinburgh case study cluster is comprised of three partnerships. The Edinburgh Capital City Partnership (CCP) is a city-wide partnership focused on area regeneration and social inclusion within the local authority boundary. It was established in 1995 in response to the government regeneration programme, Programme for Partnership. Led by the City of Edinburgh Council, CCP involves other public sector agencies and community, voluntary and private sector organisations. The North Edinburgh Area Renewal Partnership (NEAR) was launched in 1993 independently of any government funding programmes, although it is now a government-designated Social Inclusion Partnership. NEAR has developed a comprehensive regeneration agenda for this large area of public sector housing and is part of the overall area regeneration framework for Edinburgh through its connection to the Capital City Partnership. Led by the City of Edinburgh Council, its membership has expanded over time and involves a range of public agencies together with community and private sector partners. The Pilton Partnership has the same area focus as NEAR, but is focused primarily on community development and poverty issues. Established with an elaborate board structure in 1990 in response to the European Union's Poverty 3 Programme, the partnership has evolved into a joint partnership between local councillors and community organisations. It is formally and informally linked both to NEAR and to CCP.

Edinburgh's partnerships: key issues

- Edinburgh's relative affluence has meant that area regeneration has not enjoyed the same degree of priority here as in a number of the other case study regions and cities. Regeneration has tended not to feature prominently on the agendas of agencies, and the Edinburgh Capital City Partnership (CCP), established to develop a city-wide framework for regeneration, was initially conceived of as mainly a vehicle for spending specific regeneration resources, rather than for bending mainstream budgets and integrating regeneration activity with other city-wide issues. However, by late 1998 the need to integrate regeneration with other city development issues had become clear, along with the need to rethink how regeneration could move from being a special to a mainstream activity.

- The case study demonstrates the capacity of post hoc city-wide partnership structures to energise already established local partnerships. The NEAR partnership, for example, benefited as the city strategy pushed regeneration on to the agendas of public agencies, leading to a more holistic approach to the development of North Edinburgh as agencies with health and employment remits, for example, were pulled into the process.

- Further, the process by which the city strategy was developed involved 'bottom-up' inputs from local partnerships as well inputs from players with a city-wide remit, suggesting that the city regeneration framework represents, at least in part, the outcome of dialogue between local and city interests. However, one consequence of this inclusive approach to developing the strategy, was that it soon became apparent that prioritisation and streamlining would be necessary in order for it to be translated into action.

- There appears to be real progress in developing a genuine multi-level governance framework for regeneration in the city. Vertical integration is attempted through formal systems: the involvement of representatives from local partnerships as directors of the board of CCP, the inclusion of reports from local partnerships as standing items on CCP's agenda, and the development of monitoring and evaluation systems which balance city and local targets. Integration is also realised through the substantial overlap of the individuals involved. The nature and extent of vertical linkages between regeneration partnerships in Edinburgh was unusual in comparison with other case study clusters.

- The two local partnerships in the cluster operate at the same spatial scale across the same geographical area, although with distinctive remits. Thus, while NEAR has a comprehensive regeneration agenda, the Pilton Partnership is focused on community development and anti-poverty measures. The potential for confusion, duplication and even conflict between the two local partnerships might be anticipated. However, these problems have been virtually avoided through a strategic approach to subsidiarity, the sharing credit and the involvement of a number of key individuals in both partnerships.

Lanarkshire

Lanarkshire is an old industrial area comprised of a number of sizeable towns to the east and south of Glasgow. The region has suffered a sustained economic collapse similar to that of Glasgow, with the closure of the Ravenscraig steelworks in Motherwell typical of the region's problems. However, over the past few years, Lanarkshire has been successful in attracting some high-profile inward investors. Despite this, problems in the area remain significant, with severe concentrations of disadvantage.

The three partnerships in the cluster were as follows. The Lanarkshire Alliance links the two Lanarkshire local authorities established with the reorganisation of local government in Scotland, North Lanarkshire Council and South Lanarkshire Council, in a strategic regional partnership involving the Lanarkshire Development Agency, Scottish Homes and the Lanarkshire Health Board. Led by the Lanarkshire Development Agency and launched in 1997, the main focus of the Alliance is on economic development, although it also has social and environmental aims.

The North Lanarkshire Partnership is led by North Lanarkshire Council and operates strategic partnerships across the local authority area. Established in 1997 in the wake of the formation of the Lanarkshire Alliance, it involves a range of public agencies around a broad economic, social and environmental agenda. A decision will be taken on whether to expand membership to the community and private sectors once the partnership is established.

At a local level, the Motherwell North Social Inclusion Partnership was also launched in 1997, having been created to compete for the central government regeneration programme, Programme for Partnership. Led by North Lanarkshire Council, and involving public agencies alongside community, voluntary sector and private sector organisations, the partnership is concerned with the regeneration of four disadvantaged areas in Motherwell.

North Lanarkshire's partnerships: key issues

- The Lanarkshire Alliance is focused around a 'Changing Gear' strategic framework, produced in part as a response to local government reorganisation which brought about the need to 'renegotiate' pre-existing partnership arrangements. The purpose of the Alliance is to develop 'strategic alignment' between the strategies of the partners and the Changing Gear framework. A key rationale for the partnership would seem to be joined-up government at the strategic level, although the partnership has also established development groups charged with translating strategic aims into actions. In the two years since establishment, the most significant progress so far is on the development of the strategy, with working groups to take forward implementation. A monitoring framework is under development, and there is broad agreement of the types of changes the partnership will want to measure.

- The North Lanarkshire Partnership was set up in the wake of the Lanarkshire Alliance and at the instigation of the North Lanarkshire Council, which wanted a body of partners to help implement North Lanarkshire Council's strategy. In the early stages of the partnership an 'Accord' was signed up to by the partners which set out seven 'key functions' for the partnership, but this was followed by a period of delay in developing the partnership and strategy, partly caused by political issues unconnected to the partnership within North Lanarkshire Council. At the time of the research this partnership had yet to build a public profile, and there was a recognition that much work would be required before the partnership began to influence the mainstream activities of partners.

- Since its inception in 1997 in response to Programme for Partnership, the Motherwell North PPA has invested a significant degree of effort into developing a role and remit for itself and in thinking through how it could be made to work in an effective way. A key issue for the partnership has been how it can broaden its focus from assessing and approving applications for the Programme for Partnership to a wider strategic remit, and how it can widen its membership to beyond officers from public agencies and community representatives. In particular, it is likely that, in order to take on a wider strategic role and develop its profile, the partnership will need to secure the support of local politicians.

- Integration between the three partnerships in the cluster is progressing, albeit without any routine reporting or formal communication. Thus, there is felt to be coherence between the aims and objectives of the partnerships, with the Lanarkshire Alliance's Changing Gear strategy providing an overall framework, although the extent to which lower-level partnerships are viewed as a delivery mechanism for the strategy is the subject of debate: "The consistency is there, but the communication could be improved".

- The three Lanarkshire partnerships have all been established too recently for any firm conclusions to be drawn about their progress and likely effectiveness. The teething troubles that each have experienced appear not to endanger the development of a culture of partnership in the region, and there appears to be some progress towards the development of trust and respect between partners.